TIBETAN BUDDHISM

From the Ground Up

TIBETAN BUDDHISM

From the Ground Up

A Practical Approach for Modern Life

by

B. ALAN WALLACE

with Steven Wilhelm

WISDOM PUBLICATIONS ❧ BOSTON ❧ MASSACHUSETTS

WISDOM PUBLICATIONS
361 NEWBURY STREET
BOSTON, MASSACHUSETTS 02115

ISBN 0-86171-075-4

Library of Congress Cataloging-in-Publication Data

Wallace, B. Alan.
  Tibetan Buddhism from the ground up: a practical approach for
modern life / by B. Alan Wallace with Steven Wilhelm. — 1st ed.
    p.   cm.
  Includes bibliographical references and index.
  ISBN 0-86171-075-4
    1. Buddhism.   I. Wilhelm, Steven, 1948- . II. Title.
BQ4132.W35 1992   93-15120
294.3'923--dc20   CIP

98   97   96

6   5   4   3

Set in Mona Lisa Recut and Diacritical Garamond at Wisdom Publications by
Andrew Fearnside & Andrea Thompson

Designed by: L·J·SAWLiť

Printed at Northeast Impressions, Fairfield, NJ   USA

Dedicated to
My Parents and Teachers

The publisher wishes to thank the Barry Hershey Foundation for sponsoring this book.

CONTENTS

PREFACE

The following is an edited version of a series of lectures I gave in Seattle, Washington in 1988 beginning with the most basic teachings of Tibetan Buddhism and progressing gradually to more subtle theories and advanced practices. These lectures were intended as a practical introduction to Buddhism, based on my own studies, experience, and teachings I had received over the past eighteen years from teachers from all four orders of Tibetan Buddhism. Two of these lectures, appearing here as Chapters Ten and Eleven, are based on Buddhist writings preserved in the Pali language. Although these writings are not part of the Tibetan tradition, they are compatible with it, and I have drawn on them because of their exceptional usefulness and clarity.

This book is not designed as an academic introduction to Tibetan Buddhism, but rather as a straightforward guide to practice. I am hoping it will be accessible and helpful to a broad reading public, especially to those with no background in Buddhism at all.

I would like to thank my many friends in Seattle who transcribed these lectures, especially Pauly Fitze. I would also like to express my gratitude to Michael Bristol, Stuart and Sandy Baird, and Grace Watson, who have contributed to my work so generously over the years.

I would also like to thank Steven Wilhelm, a professional journalist and long-time friend, without whom this work might never have been brought to completion. During 1989, I did the initial editing of the transcripts of the first nine lectures, and Steven further polished this work. Transcripts of the final seven lectures were initially edited by Steven Wilhelm, then I edited further the entire manuscript. Finally, I am most grateful to Connie Miller and Vincent and Maria Montenegro at Wisdom Publications for their excellent work on the manuscript.

I hope the personal style of this book will provide enjoyable and meaningful reading for those interested in understanding Tibetan Buddhism in the context of the modern world.

1

Dharma and the Rituals of Happiness

Tibetan Buddhism is one of the many spiritual traditions that has evolved from the words taught by the historical Buddha some 2,500 years ago. *Dharma*, a Sanskrit word for which there is no adequate English equivalent, refers to the understanding and behavior that lead to the elimination of suffering and its source and to the experience of a lasting state of happiness and fulfillment. The Dharma taught by the Buddha is known as the *Buddhadharma*. Thus, we can describe Dharma as a way of life, a practice that can be relevant and useful to everyone, to so-called religious people and nonreligious people alike. Why? Because it tells us how to satisfy a longing we have always had, that is, the fundamental desire to experience a lasting state of happiness and to be completely free of suffering and discontent. In short, the practice of Dharma provides a means to the attainment of this goal.

Śāntideva, a seventh-century Indian Buddhist sage, writes:

> Although we wish to cast off grief,
> We hasten after misery;
> And though we long for happiness,
> Out of ignorance we crush our joy,
>   as if it were our enemy.[1]

We wish for happiness, yet frequently we fail to identify its source. We wish to be free of suffering, frustration, and grief, but we do not correctly identify the sources of our unhappiness. So, although we wish to be free of misery we hasten after it, all the while destroying the causes of the happiness we could have.

How then do we go about practicing Dharma correctly? First we must clearly understand what is not Dharma, so we can eliminate all those activities of our lives that create the causes contrary to our happiness.

THE EIGHT WORLDLY CONCERNS

Only Dharma, and a motivation appropriate to the practice of Dharma, effectively leads to fulfillment. All other activities are included in what Buddhists call the *eight worldly concerns*. These concerns dominate a life without Dharma and prevent us from entering a way of life that leads to the cessation of discontent. These eight worldly concerns are: gain and loss, pleasure and pain, praise and blame, and fame and disgrace.

These are the concerns that pervade most people's daily lives. They are pervasive precisely because they are mistaken for effective means to attain happiness and to avoid suffering. For example, many of us, driven by the concerns of gain and loss, work to acquire an income so that we can buy the things that money can buy, some of them necessities but often many of them unnecessary things that we believe will bring us happiness. We also earn money so that we can avoid the misery and humiliation of poverty.

Again, experiencing pleasure and avoiding pain are the primary motivations for a majority of our activities. We engage in many actions—some of which may seem spiritual—for the sake of immediate satisfaction or relief. For example, if we have a headache we may take aspirin, or sit and meditate hoping the headache will go away. These remedies may lead to temporary relief from discomfort, but that is where their effectiveness ends.

Praise and blame is the next pair of worldly concerns, and even a little reflection reveals the great extent to which our behavior is influenced by desire for praise and fear of blame. The final pair, fame and disgrace, includes seeking others' approval, affection, acknowledgment, respect, and appreciation, and avoiding the corresponding disapproval, rejection, and so on.

The reason for drawing attention to these eight worldly concerns is not to show that they are inherently bad. It is not bad to buy a car, enjoy a fine meal, to be praised for one's work, or be respected by others. Rather, the reason for pointing them out is to reveal their essentially transient nature and their impotence as means to lasting happiness.

Let us take the example of going on vacation. First of all, in order to perform the ritual of going on vacation, we have to save the money to pay for it. Having done this we then go to a travel agent who shows us attractive brochures, of Hawaii let's say. We look at photographs of beautiful people basking on a beach looking like they're having a wonderful time. Attracted to this formula of happiness, we pay for a facsimile of the advertised experience, and very soon we find ourselves on our way to Hawaii.

Our vacation lasts one week, and in fact we do enjoy ourselves, but naturally we must return to our homes, our jobs, and our responsibilities. The vacation is over. We want to re-live its pleasurable events, so we tell our friends about it. If we prolong this ritual, subjecting our friends to our slide shows or videos, we may meet with resistance. Then we realize it is time to stop juicing the memory of the vacation. The memory gradually fades and the relaxation vanishes as well. The vacation is over, so we settle back into the routine of our ordinary lives, until it is time to plan for the next vacation.

That is when things go well. Often, though, our plans go awry. We perform the ritual of some activity that was intended to bring us pleasure, and it fails. While our plans were meant to give us happiness, instead in the end they yield aggravation.

Finally, we find that our efforts to acquire material gain, status, praise, and fame are futile, and can lead to greater unhappiness than we started with. Depression may set in, and if we can find someone to blame for our lack of success, we may do so. This ultimately leads to conflict and turmoil with those around us. In short, dedication to the eight worldly concerns holds no promise of giving us any lasting satisfaction, and guarantees unrelenting discontent and frustration.

As we come to recognize this condition more and more clearly, it becomes natural to begin seeking alternatives, a search that may lead us to Dharma. This does not mean only applying oneself to certain spiritual exercises, but begins with a fundamental transformation of one's thinking and consequently one's way of life—avoiding unwholesome behavior and activities, and adopting those that are wholesome.

The foundation and initial goal of this transformation is avoiding doing harm to others. Whether alone or with others, we must strive to avoid doing harm either directly with our words or deeds or indirectly with our thoughts and intentions. We may injure others with abuse, slander, sarcasm, and deceit, or by acts of omission due to insensitivity and thoughtlessness. The most subtle way of harming others is indirectly by means of our thoughts, judgments, and attitudes. When the mind is dominated by hostility, we may be viciously attacking others with our thoughts. Although no apparent injury may be inflicted, these thoughts affect us internally and influence our way of interacting with others, and the long-term effect is invariably harmful. So the initial theme of Dharma practice is a nonviolent approach to our own lives, to other living beings, and to our environment. This is a foundation for spiritual practice, and can provide well-being for both ourselves and others.

On this basis of nonviolence we can look for ways to serve others keeping in mind that any work will be altruistic if our motivation is one of kindness and friendliness.

Dharma and Its Imitations

Let us focus now on other rituals that are widely regarded as spiritual practices, or Dharma: meditation, prayer, yoga, and so on. As we engage in such actions it is essential to repeatedly ask ourselves, "Are these practices motivated by the eight worldly concerns?" This point is illustrated by a well-known Tibetan story.

A man living about a thousand years ago felt dissatisfied with his life, and so he decided to practice Dharma. Tibetans on the whole are a very pious, devout people, so it was quite natural for him to apply himself to a devotional practice. A common Tibetan custom is to chant *mantras,* or prayers, while walking around a reliquary, counting the mantras with a rosary held in the left hand, and rotating a prayer wheel in the right.

While our devotee was doing this, a sage named Drom Tönpa[2] noted his behavior and commented to him, "It is very good to circumambulate a reliquary, but it is even better to practice Dharma."

We can imagine this fellow being a bit ruffled at the teacher's remark, for he clearly thought that he was practicing Dharma. But then he may have thought to himself, "A simple act of piety is apparently not enough. I'd better practice Dharma by studying the scriptures." Later on while he was pursuing this new ritual, Drom Tönpa came upon him and remarked, "It is very good to read the scriptures, but it is even better to practice Dharma."

Knowing that such studies were a commonly respected practice in Tibet, our seeker was probably more perplexed than before. But he gave the matter further thought and came upon the bright idea that he hoped would resolve the problem—Meditate! Certainly many Buddhist sages assert that meditation is the essence of Dharma, so here was a sure track. But when Drom Tönpa saw him meditating, he gently rebuked him saying, "It is very good to meditate, but it is even better to practice Dharma."

At this point our devotee-turned-scholar-turned-meditator felt exasperated. What were his options now? What did this renowned teacher have in mind? So finally he asked him, and the teacher replied, "Give up attachment to this life and let your mind become Dharma."

Devotion, scholarship, and meditation can all be empty rituals, and whether these devotional acts or any other practices are in fact Dharma depends solely upon one's motivation. What did Drom Tönpa mean when he said, "Give up attachment to this life"? He meant, give up attachment to the eight worldly concerns; let them no longer govern the way you live your life.

"Let your mind become Dharma," encouraged Drom Tönpa. Our initial attempts at spiritual practice tend to be very self-conscious. We want to overcome the distortions of our minds and cultivate such wholesome qualities as kindness, insight, mindfulness, and concentration; but as we engage in practices designed to cultivate these, at first they appear to be only mental exercises. Dharma seems separate, something adopted from outside. But as we go deeper into the practice, this sense of separation begins to disappear; our minds become the very Dharma we seek to cultivate.

It is quite easy to understand the eight worldly concerns on an intellectual level, but it is far more difficult to identify them in the course of our spiritual practice. I recall a striking comment made by a Tibetan contemplative friend. He became a monk at age seven, received sound, extensive training in Dharma from superb teachers while in his twenties, and subsequently went into solitary retreat in a small hut in the mountains above Dharamsala, India. For years he devoted himself to meditation, leading a life of simplicity and poverty for the sake of his spiritual practice. However, after almost twenty years of such efforts, he commented to me that his first several years in retreat were actually an embodiment of the eight worldly concerns, something he was totally oblivious to at the time. The infiltration of these concerns, which makes a mockery of Dharma, is subtle indeed!

Cultivating the mind is very much like cultivating a crop. A farmer must know the proper way to prepare the soil, sow the seed, tend to the growth of the crop, and finally harvest it. If all these tasks are done properly, the farmer will reap the best harvest that nature allows. If they're done improperly, an inferior harvest will be produced, regardless of the farmer's hopes and anxieties.

Similarly, in terms of meditation it is crucial to be thoroughly versed in the proper method of our chosen technique. While engaged in the practice, we must frequently check up to see whether we are implementing the instructions we have heard and conceptually understood. Like a good crop, good meditation cannot be forced, and requires cultivation over time.

Let me illustrate this subtle domination of the eight worldly concerns by an example from my own experience. During the early 1970s, I was a young student of Buddhism living in Dharamsala. This mountain village in northern India is the headquarters of His Holiness the Dalai Lama, the spiritual and temporal leader of the Tibetans, and is also home to several thousand Tibetan refugees, many of them monks, nuns, and Lamas. Because I had begun my studies of the Tibetan language and Buddhism in a Western university and quickly found excellent opportunities for further training in Dharamsala, I soon came to be regarded as one of the more knowledgeable Western students—even after I had been there only several months. At times this reputation led me to a sense of personal superiority or specialness. I noted this deluded attitude, and it concerned me: If after just a little training I was already feeling self-righteous, was I doomed to increasing arrogance in proportion to my expanding knowledge and experience?

It was while I was concerned with this problem that I was granted my first audience with His Holiness the Dalai Lama, whom I asked for advice. His Holiness responded with an analogy: "Imagine that you are very hungry and you are given a full plate of delicious, nourishing food. After satisfying your hunger, would you congratulate yourself on your prowess at eating? Would you feel self-righteous?" "Surely not," I answered. And he continued: "It's the same with Dharma. You've come here with a yearning to be free

7

of discontent and to find true satisfaction. You've come seeking Dharma, and your desire is being fulfilled. There's no more reason to feel self-righteous about this experience than about the accomplishment of eating a good meal."

His Holiness went on to speak of his own situation. He referred to himself simply as Tenzin Gyatso, a Buddhist monk who has been well educated in the long-term consequences of ethically wholesome and unwholesome actions.

"Now think of the behavior of a housefly," he said. "It is simply concerned with such things as getting food, and it acts with selfish desire which easily turns to aggression when it must compete with others. Is it appropriate for me to feel contemptuous of the fly for its behavior? Surely not, for it doesn't know any better. Likewise, it is inappropriate to disdain other people for their harmful behavior, especially if they have not learned the distinction between wholesome and unwholesome actions. However, if I, who have been well taught in this regard, should act like those who have not, this would be shameful. Greater understanding properly leads to an increasing sense of responsibility, and not to arrogance."

SIGNS OF DHARMA PRACTICE

As we enter the practice of Dharma, we may be in for some disappointing surprises. We learn how to identify the arising of mental distortions in daily life and the unwholesome behavior that ensues from them. In this learning process we may find that our minds, and our way of life, are far less wholesome than we had previously thought. Many beginning Dharma students remark that before they began practicing Buddhism they had thought of themselves as fairly wise and friendly people; but after examining their own behavior more carefully, they were dismayed at the unwholesome quality of their lives. This discovery may seriously threaten our self-esteem. Finding it difficult to accept certain traits in our own makeup, we may find ourselves compulsively seeking out and dwelling on these same faults in others. For example, if we especially abhor our own tendency to self-righteousness, we may be scathing in our contempt of others whom we perceive as exhibiting this quality. For this reason, quite frequently people in the early stages of Dharma practice find the company of others very painful, because they see their own faults mirrored in the behavior of others and, of course, this all appears quite disagreeable. A little understanding can be a painful thing, but this discomfort is eased not by withdrawing from Dharma practice, but by persevering in it and cultivating deeper insight and compassion.

What are the signs that we are properly cultivating Dharma in our lives? Serenity and good cheer are qualities to look for. These characteristics reflect a type of awareness that maintains equilibrium through good and bad times alike. In the face of adversity the Dharma practitioner does not fall into despair, nor does he respond with elation or anxious clinging when he meets with good fortune. Instead, he accepts them both with equanimity.

This equanimity is not a sign of apathy or passivity. On the contrary, it is an attitude of calm cheerfulness that is as prepared for action as it is for repose. It is a sense of well-being that is neither produced by pleasurable external stimuli, nor is it diminished by adversity. Its source is the increasing sanity of our own minds brought forth by the practice of Dharma.

The core of Dharma practice is freeing oneself from the attachments of this life. It focuses on the deeper issue of gaining complete release from discontent by means of freeing our minds from the afflictions of confusion, attachment, and anger. In a broader sense, Dharma practice is concerned with serving others, in terms of both their temporary and ultimate needs.

Does this mean that one who is committed to Dharma suddenly renounces all worldly enjoyments—no more vacations, no entertainment, no sensory pleasures? No. If one tries that approach it usually results in spiritual burnout; and the common rebound is equally extreme sensual indulgence.

For this reason, the practice of Buddhist Dharma is often called the *Middle Way* because it seeks to avoid the extremes of sensual indulgence and severe asceticism. The former leads to perpetual dissatisfaction and the latter damages one's physical and mental health. Both are foreign to Dharma. To deny ourselves such enjoyments will most likely retard our spiritual growth, for our practice will take on a flavor of deprivation and frustration.

The Middle Way is a sensitive exertion of effort that is neither lax nor aggressive, and from this practice there ultimately arises an increasing satisfaction and delight in virtuous activity that is a result of our spiritual transformation.

As we grow in Dharma, the need for such external sources of pleasure is bound to recede, for we become nourished by a sense of well-being arising from the depths of our own minds. This transition is gradual and cannot be forced. The path of Dharma is meant to be a joyful one, of increasing inner satisfaction, and decreasing need for pleasurable external stimulation.

2

LIFE'S OLDEST ILLUSION

As long as our minds are dominated by the eight worldly concerns, we are bound to remain in a state of dissatisfaction,
always vulnerable to grief and fear. Our life is like a tiny boat drifting far out at sea; every wave, every peak and trough, disturbs our
equilibrium, and any great wave can overturn our world. So we are
faced with the question: How can we create greater emotional stability through alleviating the afflictions of our minds? One way is to
confront and overcome what might be called life's oldest illusion—
the illusion about our own mortality.

THE RESULTS OF IGNORING DEATH

All of us acknowledge that one day we will die. In fact, some people
maintain that human beings are the only creatures capable of
anticipating their own death. Although we have this ability, most
of us stifle it as much as we can. We avoid thinking about our own
mortality, and when the subject does come up, we tend to think,
"Of course I will die, but not today, or at least not in the near
future." Death is pushed away into the nebulous distant future, just
far enough so that it does not appear threatening and does not
influence the way we live. In this way we ignore a crucial facet of
life—the fact that life ends. By so doing we create an illusion of
immortality.

One result of adhering to the illusion of immortality is that we
become enmeshed in the chain of trivial concerns that fill daily life.
We apply ourselves wholeheartedly to the eight worldly concerns,

with the result that we become continually battered about by mental afflictions and the unwholesome behavior that ensues from them.

In leading such a life, we may feel some dissatisfaction—especially when things are not going well—and this may generate the aspiration to engage in spiritual practice. But our efforts are bound to be feeble and intermittent and often just another expression of the mundane concern for temporary relief from dissatisfaction. We will just be looking for another quick fix, whether through meditation, attending church or temple, or engaging in devotions.

The illusion of immortality is always accompanied by grasping onto reality as if it were unchanging. Naturally we feel that we have individual personal identities that are relatively stable even while our minds and bodies are in a state of flux. We realize that our emotions change, our thoughts shift, our views fluctuate, and our bodies feel different from hour to hour, but we believe that the "I" who experiences these changing events remains essentially the same.

Adhering to this deluded belief in an immutable ego, we ignore the fact that everyone's nature is impermanent; so too are our personal relationships and circumstances. All these are subject to change. The subtle changes in our environment may also pass unnoticed. Operating with such a deeply imbued fantasy of immutability, we are vulnerable to any stark changes that may demand our attention: the death of a loved one, the loss of income, the discovery that we are seriously ill, and so on. Such changes are bound to throw us into emotional turmoil, as our carefully nurtured illusion of security, based upon imaginary stability, is suddenly threatened.

With this fantasy of security we try to keep our own death at a safe distance thinking, "I shall die, but not so soon that it should affect the way I live now." While maintaining this conviction, we still may feel an urge to practice Dharma, once we have learned that this is an option; but we postpone earnest practice to an indefinite time in the future when we are not so busy.

As long as we ignore our inevitable death and the absolute uncertainty of the time when it will occur, we feel free to indulge in pointless talk and in being preoccupied with food, drink, and other sensual pleasures. Strong craving arises for material acquisitions and prestige, and we become infuriated when we encounter obstacles. Thus, the ignorance, pride, jealousy, and other afflictions this denial causes dominate our minds relentlessly; and these incite behavior that brings us more misery both in the near and far future.

THE RESULTS OF CULTIVATING AWARENESS OF DEATH

Cultivating awareness of impermanence and death is crucial for discarding the eight worldly concerns and for entering Dharma. For this reason the Buddha declared that among all realizations, that of impermanence and death is the greatest.

With this awareness, a radical shift occurs in our view of life and in our priorities. Recognizing our inevitable parting from our loved ones and possessions, attachment to them wanes; and concern for material gain, acknowledgment, and prestige is blown away like chaff in the wind. Having cast aside these mundane concerns, we are definitely in a position to practice Dharma wholeheartedly and with enthusiasm. Because of its powerful impact upon the way we lead our lives, mindfulness of death is vital at all stages of spiritual practice.

Imagine starting a close relationship with another person, while maintaining full awareness of our own and that other person's mortality. This would most certainly change the relationship. The truth is, as soon as two individuals meet, parting is inevitable. In this regard, Śāntideva tells us:

> Casting all aside, I must depart alone.
> But not knowing this, I have engaged in
> Various nonvirtuous deeds
> On account of friend and foe.

But my foes shall cease to exist,
Friends shall vanish,
I, too, will perish,
So will everything pass from existence.[3]

The recognition of impermanence can prevent a great deal of anxiety and grief that arises from attachment and from insisting that pleasant conditions remain as they are. This awareness encourages a light touch, preventing us from grasping too hard at possessions, status, and the like.

An awakening to the reality of one's own death may lead to widely divergent results for different people. If this occurs to someone with no spiritual awareness, it may well lead to intensified hedonism and frenzied grasping. When this realization occurs to someone whose life is consumed by trivialities, it merely emphasizes the meaninglessness of their condition.

But the same realization occurring to a spiritually aware person will enrich that person's mind. He suddenly recognizes that his present body is on loan, and that all his relationships with other people are temporary. This insight into the inevitability of death, and the fact that it may come at any time, causes him to ask, "How can I make this human life and my relationships with others as meaningful as possible?"

If we look at the mind and find that it is dominated by resentment, selfish desire, jealousy, conceit, and other distortions, and if we see that our lives are permeated with unwholesome behavior, then fear of death is justified. An afflicted, unwholesome life is bound to lead to an afflicted, unwholesome death; and if individual experience is to continue after death, then the unwholesomeness will naturally follow as well. Fearing death in itself is pointless—why be afraid of something that is inevitable? But fear of such an unwholesome death can be useful, because it may impel us to improve the quality of our life, and consequently avoid such a fear-ridden death.

This anxiety about death may be likened to the fear felt by a person who has ingested a poison for which there is a known, available antidote. A useful response, motivated by fear, would be to find the remedy as soon as possible. A ridiculous reaction to such a discovery would be to dismiss it as morbid and to seek some inane form of distraction.

If there were nothing that could be done to alter the nature of one's death and any post-death experience, we would have to accept it as inescapable. However, while the fact of death cannot be altered, the nature of our experience of death and what follows can be transformed. The experience may be miserable and barren, or it may be blissful and fulfilling. The Buddhist view is simple: nonvirtuous behavior leads to misery; virtuous behavior leads to joy.

There is a saying in the Tibetan Buddhist tradition: It is better to fear death now and die fearlessly, than to avoid fear of death now and die with terror. Particularly if we are aware that it is possible to lead a meaningful life in Dharma and yet fail to do so, our own death is bound to be encountered with remorse. In the final moments we will realize our life has been a series of meaningless activities, leading nowhere but to suffering, with the opportunity to transform it lost.

CULTIVATING MINDFULNESS OF DEATH

How can we cultivate an awareness of death that invigorates and purifies our practice of Dharma? This can be done by means of sequential, discursive meditation. The first subject of meditation is to reflect on the inevitability of our own death. We can quickly recognize this on a purely intellectual level, but it takes time to let the full import of this reality sink in. When we see or hear of someone else's death, we tend to take the role of spectator, as if dying were for other people.

This reminds me of a story I once heard about an aborigine in

Australia who committed a crime and was sentenced to death by hanging. When he learned of his punishment, the aborigine was stunned and pleaded with the authorities, "You can't hang me! Hanging is for white people—they're used to it!" Isn't it true that semiconsciously we believe, "Death is for other people—the old, the diseased, the poor—they're used to it"?

Each of us will meet with death. We may do so with courage or with trepidation. The experience of dying may be painful or exhilarating, profound or trivial. However we experience it, it will certainly take place, whether or not we feel we are ready. Even if we enjoy a long life, there will come a time when the body simply wears out. The heart begins to fail, the kidneys no longer function, circulation becomes poor, and breathing occurs only with difficulty. We may go to the finest doctors in the world, receive the best medical treatment technology has to offer, attend carefully to our diet and exercise; but finally there will be nothing more that we can do. Our time will be up. Even the greatest individuals in history—including those of great spiritual attainment—died. So, too, will each of us meet with death.

Not only is death unavoidable, but with each second our life span is running out. Our days are numbered, and that number diminishes from the moment we are conceived. There is no pause in this movement, and there is no way to turn the clock back once we realize we have been wasting this precious time.

The second subject in the meditation on death is the most potent: that the time of our death is absolutely uncertain. Some people die while still in their mother's womb, some die at birth, others in childhood or youth, others in the prime of life, and yet others in old age. The world presents myriad conditions that can result in our immediate death, so our lives may come to an end while enjoying superb health, great prosperity, and supposed security.

This point is well illustrated by an account I recently heard of a relatively young woman. On a Friday she began to feel ill, and the next night she went to the emergency room with a cough. They told her to go home and rest. When she felt worse the next day she returned, but they sent her home with antibiotics. On Sunday she returned a third time, and this time they admitted her. By that Wednesday night she was dead of a staph pneumonia that had eaten up her lungs. She was thirty-five, and until shortly before her death she seemed to be perfectly healthy.

Modern technology has found ways to combat a number of diseases, but it has also strengthened the power of many of its old foes. Furthermore, we have now so polluted our environment that it becomes increasingly dangerous to breathe, drink water, or eat food. We continue to upset the balance of the rare conditions that support human life on our planet, and in so doing we make ourselves more and more vulnerable to premature death. The human body, while extraordinarily resilient in some respects, is also extremely fragile. The possibility of death is never far away.

How can we maintain awareness of imminent death and remain engaged in the world, going to work, caring for family, and so on? When skillfully introduced into daily life, mindfulness of death does not clutter our minds with morbid thoughts or prevent us from leading healthy lives. It does, however, take the wind out of the sails of the eight worldly concerns. It helps us to lighten up, so that we are not so weighed down with anxiety and frustration about the minor vicissitudes of daily living.

The third and final subject of this meditation raises the question: What is of real value in the face of death? Throughout our lives we may cherish our friendships, family ties, romances, possessions, and pleasant memories. But the passage of death is one that each of us makes alone, and all loved ones, belongings, and memories of pleasures are left behind. Whether we have had an enjoyable life or a miserable one, death severs us from all previous objects of joy and sorrow. With the deterioration of neural activity during the dying process, even our thoughts and emotions vanish. What, then, in the face of death is meaningful and worthwhile? Only Dharma will be of benefit.

Dharma is often defined as that which is truly of benefit at the time of death. This would not be so if death meant total annihilation of the individual and all experience. But the Buddha and many other contemplatives have discovered there is a continuity of awareness beyond death. This continuity does not depend upon an individual's belief system. Whether or not we believe it, there is no final extinction of individual consciousness at death.

This continuing consciousness is not an anonymous stream of raw awareness. Rather, it carries innumerable impressions from an individual's past experiences, as well as personal characteristics and behavior patterns. If this stream of consciousness is heavily laden with imprints from mental distortions and nonvirtuous behavior, misery follows death. Virtuous impressions, on the other hand, ripen into experiences of joy and contentment. Thus, the only thing that carries on after death is our stream of impression-laden consciousness, and it is Dharma that creates the causes for those imprints to be of a beneficial nature. A life devoid of Dharma brings dissatisfaction here and now, and leads to suffering in later lives.

Meditation on death can transform our lives. Some of us may have had the good fortune to have experienced a brush with death, an event that may often invigorate our Dharma practice. This happened to me when I was twenty-three-years old. A few years earlier, I was studying the Tibetan language at a university in Germany, with plans to go to India to learn Buddhism from Tibetan Lamas living there as refugees. But a friend warned me against going. He had seen a world map with regions of land painted various colors corresponding to the types of disease that prevail in them; and the coloration of India was positively psychedelic. But I was determined to go, and during my four-year stay there, I experienced a colorful array of illnesses. My second year in India was almost my last, for a combination of jaundice, malnutrition, and parasites came close to terminating my life.

I was living in a Tibetan monastery, with no access to any hospital care, although I was taking Tibetan medication. There were thirty monks in the monastery, two of them my roommates, and all of us living barely at the subsistence level. Seeing that all that could be done for me had been done, my fellow monks continued in their daily activities of devotions and study. It seemed very odd to me that their lives should carry on as usual while I was evidently dying. They would often ask me how I was doing, but I found it difficult to answer. What could I say, "I'm dying, how are you doing?" It seemed obvious that life would carry on, but it would have no place for me. I would be missed by my friends and family, but the memory would gradually fade and I would be forgotten.

Prior to this experience, I had occasionally thought that since one day I would have to die, it would be nice to go in my sleep. There was a pleasant fantasy of drifting painlessly from one sort of slumber to another. But as my health rapidly deteriorated, the prospect lost all appeal. On three or four successive nights I went to sleep realizing that I might never wake up, and during one of those nights the initial phase of death, according to Tibetan Buddhist tradition, did in fact begin. But, due to the intervention of a Tibetan doctor and a Tibetan holy man, I pulled out, my health turned around, and I recovered. I had come very close to dying, and this prospect had filled me with dismay, for I was dissatisfied with the quality of my Dharma practice. As I began to recover, there came a point at which I no longer felt that I was about to die. But I truly saw that death had not been averted, only postponed.

Cultivating mindfulness of death acts as a potent stimulant for Dharma practice, and is the best antidote against the seduction of the eight worldly concerns. Meditation on impermanence and death is neither pleasant nor peaceful, nor does it have the attraction of being esoteric or mystical. It is needed, though, to counter the illusion of immortality and its many harmful effects. It can be both fascinating and rewarding to observe how the awareness of death sweeps away trivial attachments, regrets, and grievances. Moreover, such awareness creates space in our own lives for Dharma, to cultivate a way of life that yields the deep and lasting satisfaction we have been seeking all along.

3

Death: No Exit

Common Assumptions About Death

Our beliefs about death are closely related to our sense of personal identity. For example, we naturally identify with our bodies. When looking in a mirror we feel we are gazing at ourselves, a belief that drives many people to take great pains about how they appear to the world. Similarly, we identify others with their bodies, and this may contribute to our uneasiness or fear at seeing a corpse—the body is there, but the person is not. Philosophically we may then conclude that a person is only a living, conscious body. Given this premise, that life and consciousness are merely attributes produced by the physical organism, it follows that death extinguishes the person; only decomposing flesh and bone remain.

It is important to recognize that this hypothesis predates the rise of science. Although many modern scientists adopt such a view, it has never been verified by scientific means. In fact, much of biological research, for example, is conducted on the basis of this assumption without ever questioning it. The belief that purely physical events are entirely responsible for the emergence of life and consciousness is so deeply ingrained in modern science it has virtually become a matter of scientific creed.

We look out upon the world with our senses, and we perceive colors, sounds, smells, tastes, and tactile sensations. All these sensations are subjective in that they exist only in relation to our senses. What is really out there in the objective world, independent of our perceptions? Contemporary scientific materialism asserts that objective reality is composed entirely of matter and energy, and that reality has been that way since the origin of the universe.

In this scientific system awareness is an emergent property of the nervous system, and the nervous system is composed entirely of matter and energy. Scientific materialism offers quite a plausible account of the evolution from unconscious atoms and energy to the emergence of the human mind. This theory states that some point early in the history of the cosmos (if we accept the Big Bang theory), atoms formed into molecules. These molecules had new properties. A molecule such as H_2O, for instance, has qualities not found in either of its atomic components of hydrogen and oxygen, either individually or collectively. To take some of its obvious properties, water is wet at seventy degrees Fahrenheit, it freezes at thirty-two degrees, and salts will dissolve in it. These attributes, not found in the individual atoms of the water molecule, are therefore called emergent properties of those molecules.

This theory also states that during the evolution of the cosmos more and more complex molecules were created. Some of the most complex were amino acids and DNA. These, too, were simply configurations of matter and energy, but they displayed unique emergent properties due to their complex organizations. Organic molecules then combined to form single-celled organisms as well as viruses, which cannot be classified with certainty as either living or nonliving. In the former, life emerged as a property of the molecules that made up the cell. Eventually the first cells with a neurosystem, such as the hydra, evolved, and from this point we may speak of the emergent property of primitive awareness. Human consciousness with all its complexity, the theory concludes, is merely an emergent property of a far more sophisticated configuration of matter and energy, the human body, which evolved according to the laws of natural science.

Now let us return to the water molecule. If the configuration of its individual atoms is destroyed and the atoms separate, the unique properties of the molecule do not go anywhere. They simply vanish, for the organization of matter and energy from which they arose is no longer present. This is equally true, according to scientific materialism, of the emergent property of awareness—human or otherwise.

When the neurosystem ceases functioning, materialists say, awareness disappears without a trace. The implications of this view concerning the nature of death are clear: individual awareness vanishes, and only a decomposing configuration of matter and energy remain.

IS SCIENCE OBJECTIVE?

The above theory is plausible and intelligently conceived. Its proponents go on to insist, however, that it is true and that incompatible theories are "unscientific" (which is often used as a synonym for "unreasonable").

If we are to adopt that theory as objectively true, we should have a sound understanding of what is meant by energy and matter. But here we run into problems. Nobel Prize-winning physicist Richard Feynman asserts that modern science has no notion of what energy is. And while scientists believe almost unanimously in the existence of atoms, their views vary widely as to what atoms are. Some noted physicists believe they are mere properties of space, others contend they are sets of relationships, and still others, including noted physicist Werner Heisenberg, deny that they are material things at all.

Particularly when venturing into the realm of quantum mechanics, we encounter statements by leading physicists saying that not only energy, but the entire array of elementary particles, are simply constructs of our theories. Thus, physicist John Gribbin even suggests that subatomic particles did not exist until they were observed in this century.

Some scientists acknowledge our physical theories are created by the human mind, and that observations of elementary particles are functions of human awareness. So on the basis of modern physics, the seemingly backward hypothesis that the physical world of our experience is an emergent property of consciousness seems at least as plausible as the opposite view of scientific materialism. This creates problems of circularity. When energy and material particles are asserted by some physicists to be constructs of the human mind, for instance, it seems odd to maintain at the same time that the mind is a mere by-product of those same physical entities. Such questions, reaching to the very foundations of physics and science as a whole, cry out for greater understanding of the nature of consciousness. The materialist way of shrugging it off as an accidental by-product of matter and energy offers no avenue for gaining such insight. This issue is vital to understanding the animate and inanimate universe.

When it comes to understanding atoms, energy, or other natural phenomena, scientists create theories that account for observed events and make them predictable. Thanks to those theories, the phenomena now appear not as random events, but are understood as following natural laws. However, it is well known among physicists—though not widely advertised to the lay public—that two or more theories may have the same explanatory and predictive power and yet be incompatible. This fact should not deter us from creating more encompassing theories, but it should cause us to question which, if any, of our theories is true in any purely objective sense.[4]

CONSERVATION OF CONSCIOUSNESS

Although the above discussion may appear to be a lengthy diversion from our stated subject of the nature of death, it is directly relevant to the nature of consciousness, which in turn is central to the Buddhist understanding of death and its consequences. Buddhists believe there is continuity of individual consciousness after death, and that this consciousness is eventually conjoined with a new body. We are thus reborn after death, each life following the one before.

Neither in Western science nor in Western religious scripture do we have so compelling a theory of the origins and nature of consciousness. If Buddhism has anything to offer Western civilization, it may well be its profound understanding of the mind. Buddhism presents many theories about the functioning and potential of human consciousness that can be tested empirically. If these theories are finally refuted by scientific means, then the core of the Buddhist world view will be undermined. On the other hand, if many of these hypotheses are confirmed by sound and thorough empirical investigation, we may need to radically alter our interpretation of both scientific and religious knowledge.

Let us now see how a Buddhist theory of consciousness explains death. We can begin with an analogy. The central principle of modern physics is the conservation of mass-energy. This means that matter and energy may undergo innumerable transformations— from solid to liquid to gas, from thermal to electromagnetic energy, and so on—but no quantity of mass-energy is ever lost. Nor does any form of matter or energy ever arise from nothing.

In Buddhist thought we encounter a similar theory of the conservation of awareness. It says an individual's continuum of consciousness undergoes innumerable changes—from the waking state to dreaming to deep sleep, from emotional turbulence to serenity, and so on—but awareness never vanishes. Nor does consciousness ever arise from nothing.

The Buddhist view is that mass-energy does not transform into awareness, nor does awareness disappear into mass-energy. Mass-energy is conserved as mass-energy, and mental events, including consciousness, are conserved as mental events. Thus this theory refutes the belief that awareness originally evolved from mass-energy as an emergent property. It also denies that the awareness of a fetus arises purely from the physical conditions that produced its body. And finally it opposes the view that consciousness vanishes at death. With regard to consciousness, the Buddhist theory is compatible with much scientific evidence about cosmology, embryology, and death. However, it stands in opposition to the materialist interpretation of that evidence.

According to the Buddhist theory of the conservation of mental events, some forms of consciousness are manifest, while others are latent. For example, when you are angry about something the mental event of anger is manifest, but when you become calm again, the anger becomes latent. When you witness a beautiful sunset, your awareness of it is manifest, but afterward that awareness becomes latent. In the dream state both the waking consciousness (including sensory awareness) and the consciousness of deep sleep are latent; in the waking state dreaming awareness and deep sleep are dormant; and while in deep sleep, the dreaming and waking consciousness are latent.

Our latent impressions of mental afflictions, sensory perceptions, different states of awareness, and so on lie dormant until the appropriate conditions occur to arouse them into their manifest state. All such mental events can be radically transmuted, which allows the mind to be ultimately free of all afflictions; but throughout all such transformations the principle of conservation of awareness holds.

Buddhism asserts that all natural phenomena, including, of course, mental events, arise in dependence upon two types of causes: substantial causes and cooperative conditions. The substantial cause of a sprout of wheat, for example, is the grain of wheat from which it grows. That grain transforms into the sprout and its molecular structure determines that it will be a sprout of wheat and not, let us say, of corn. Many other conditions, including weather patterns, temperature, and farming methods may contribute to the growth of the sprout; but they do not act as the dominant, substantial cause of the grain.

Physical events arise from physical substantial causes, but their cooperative conditions may include both physical and mental events. A wheat crop may have been sown, for instance, because of a farmer's intention, and it may be irrigated because of his wish to have a profitable harvest. Intention and desire are clearly mental events and they can be instrumental in the growth of a field of wheat.

Mental events arise only from mental substantial causes, but their cooperative conditions may include both mental and physical events. Amino acids, DNA, neurological processes, diet, and environmental conditions—all these physical events—contribute to the emergence of states of awareness. But they do not play the dominant, substantial role of preceding mental functions and latent impressions.

At this point it may seem that Buddhism has returned us to an absolute dichotomy between mind and matter. It is true that this Buddhist theory refuses to subsume mind under matter or matter under mind; but it differs sharply from the type of dichotomy envisioned, for example, by Descartes.

According to Buddhism consciousness is regarded as an event, or continuum of events, rather than as a thing moving through time. Energy also can best be understood as an event, and even matter, which appears to us so "thing-ish," dissolves into a matrix of events when it is examined closely. So Buddhism is not arguing that the mental realm is just as real and tangible as the physical world appears to be. Rather, it asserts that the substantial appearance of the world of physical things is deceptive, and that both physical and mental phenomena are best understood as interdependent events. This implies that no phenomenon exists with its own intrinsic, independent identity, because each phenomenon depends on others. In Buddhism this is a key concept, which will be further discussed later.

DEATH: ANOTHER BEGINNING

What does this theory say about death, which each of us experiences? It says that death provides us with no exit from the joys and sorrows, delights and tribulations of existence.

During the death process, the body loses its ability to support human consciousness. The various sensory faculties, emotions, and thoughts retract into a latent state, and a more simple, unmodified state of awareness emerges. When consciousness is thus reduced to its primordial state, free of conceptualization, there may occur a transcendent experience of ultimate reality, if one is properly prepared for this event. Otherwise, one merely experiences a brief sense of spaciousness that is rapidly eclipsed by various types of visionary experience.

At death, the stream of awareness that departs from the body is no longer human, though it does carry a vast array of latent impressions from the just-ended life as well as from earlier lives. These impressions are responsible for the type of experiences one undergoes during the intermediate period following death and prior to the next life.

When this phase is over, if one is about to take another human rebirth, the stream of consciousness conjoins with the regenerative substances of one's parents either during or after they join in sexual union, and conception takes place. During the development of the fetus that awareness takes on the functions and attributes of human consciousness, namely, the latent impressions of human emotions, thinking, and so on are activated.

These three phases—death, intermediate period, and conception—are similar to the three states of deep sleep, dreaming, and waking. Understanding this, Tibetan contemplatives take full advantage of these states occurring during the sleeping process by practicing techniques such as dream yoga and other meditations in which awareness is gradually retracted as it is during the death process. In these practices great emphasis is placed on experiencing the state of clear light, or primordial awareness, which ordinarily manifests just before death. There are tremendous advantages to this achievement, because it helps the yogi overcome mental afflictions and obscurations, and it leads to the ability to choose one's next rebirth at will.

Buddhists believe that the type of death, intermediate period, and rebirth we experience is determined by the way we lead our lives. Each act we perform leaves impressions upon our mind-streams. Unwholesome deeds lead to suffering, wholesome acts lead to happiness and fulfillment. At death the mental continuum that has been deeply cultivated by Dharma generally begins the next rebirth endowed with a comparable degree of spiritual maturity. So it is that the path of Dharma continues from lifetime to lifetime and culminates in the perfection of complete spiritual awakening, in which one is irrevocably released from all afflictions and obscurations.

4

A Spirit of Emergence

The Thirst for Certainty

The Buddhist theory of the continuity of consciousness may be regarded as plausible, but not conclusive. One may turn away from the uncomfortable subject of death with the thought, "Who really knows anyway? The Buddhists have their view, the Christians have theirs, and the materialists have yet other theories. I'll find out about death when I experience it."

This cautious, skeptical view has its logic, and yet it is flawed, because it is not how we act in other areas of life. All of us engage in many activities, seeking happiness and wishing to avoid suffering, yet how often are we certain our efforts will bring us the satisfaction we desire? Our lives are saturated with uncertainty. As we seek an education, find employment, marry, act as parents, and plan for future economic security, we are always dealing with unknowns. And yet we forge ahead on the basis of our best judgment and intuition. We also use our best judgment about other people, institutions, our individual and national future, and the world at large, including spiritual issues. In none of these areas do we have any guarantees our beliefs are valid, but we act on them nonetheless. Otherwise we would neither be able to make decisions nor act.

If our life plans are based on best judgment, the conclusion should be clear: if we plan for our old age, it is all the more reasonable to plan for our death, since there is no certainty we will reach old age. It is almost like an investment risk: if consciousness does continue after death, and if our present actions determine the way we die and how we will live in future lives, acting as if reincarnation is true is of the greatest personal importance, and can have a deep impact on our lives.

If, on the other hand, we believe we are annihilated when we die, this also has a profound influence on the way we live. Not having thought seriously about death and the nature of consciousness, it is likely we are living as if this life is the only one we have. However, if that materialist belief is incorrect, its influence on us is bound to be unfavorable. We live in peril if we are not preparing for future lives, and the dangers do not go away by ignoring them. Nor can we live safely by taking the agnostic stance of "wait and see," for we may never be certain.

The materialist view that awareness is an accidental by-product of matter and energy that vanishes at death implies many things about the mind. This view provides little incentive for spiritual striving, for our efforts would be essentially limited by our genetic makeup and cultural and biological conditioning. Moreover, according to this belief, whatever transformations in consciousness, however meager, that might have been achieved in life would be totally snuffed out at death.

The Buddhist theory of the continuity of consciousness makes a bold statement about death and also about the nature of the mind and its role in the universe. It asserts that awareness is one of the fundamental constituents of the universe, no less essential than matter or energy, and that the potentials of awareness are just as awesome as those of any physical phenomenon. The question "What does it mean to be conscious?" now takes on cosmic significance.

If, on the basis of the evidence available to us, we tentatively conclude we will experience future lives following this one, the question needs to be posed: Is the nature of that future experience coherently related to our present way of life, or does this sequence of lives occur randomly? And if our present behavior does influence our future lives, what behavior is beneficial and what is harmful?

If we set out to find answers to these questions, we may be startled by the profusion of sources that claim such knowledge, and by the great diversity of their explanations. Mediums, clairvoyants, palmists, astrologers, psychics, mystics, and self-proclaimed enlight-ened beings—all of these and more step forward to offer us guidance. The Buddha certainly is claimed to have had experiential knowl-edge of these matters resulting from his own spiritual awakening, and Buddhists ever since have spoken with authority on the basis of the Buddha's and others' contemplative experience.

The questions we pose are important ones, but most of us do not know how to answer them on our own, or how to distinguish between teachers who speak with knowledge and those who are deluded or dishonest. Nowadays many people who wish to know about their past and future lives go to psychics and "Gurus" who claim to have access to this knowledge. Sometimes one is given answers allegedly originating from a "channeled source"—some entity whose very existence, let alone degree of knowledge, cannot be confirmed by the seeker. In other cases the information is said to be authenticated by the speaker's own clairvoyance or mystical real-ization. More often than not, the seeker has no way of knowing the origin, extent, or degree of fallibility of that knowledge.

What the Buddha Taught

The Buddha's teachings are unusual in that they explain at great length the nature of his enlightenment and the types of meditative disciplines he used to gain his insights. He left us a road map to enlightenment. Indeed, his chief motivation for teaching was to lead others to the spiritual awakening he experienced. Statements attributed to the Buddha make it very clear that all sentient beings have the capacity to become Buddhas, and that his own realiza-tions occurred by practicing the Dharma he taught. Over the past 2,500 years the Buddha's teachings have been tested experientially by thousands of the greatest sages of Asia. Many have verified for themselves the Buddha's words and have achieved the same realiza-tions he did.

The Buddha spoke extensively about the relationship between actions and their results in this and future lives. As a starting point, if we believe these teachings, we can only do so out of faith. With faith we can immediately make use of this knowledge and benefit by it. However, if we also wish to investigate the matter for ourselves, the Buddha has shown us the way to train our minds so we can experience these truths. This is a far more demanding and gradual task than simply adopting a theory, but it is also the central challenge of the Buddha's message.

The Buddha taught that our actions place impressions upon our mindstreams, and that these impressions carry on after death. Certain types of behavior leave impressions which, when stimulated in this or in future lives, result in suffering. Other types of behavior ripen into a state of well-being. These results are called the fully matured effect of the action. If the effect is painful, the causal action is said to be unwholesome, and if it is joyful, the action is wholesome. This, in short, is the Buddhist law of *karma*, which means action, and it is on this principle that Buddhist morality is based.

It is worth noting that the Buddha did not make up the dos and don'ts of Buddhist ethics; he observed the results of certain actions and reported them. The Buddha found that certain types of actions generate suffering in future lives, and these he referred to as unwholesome actions. Others generate happiness, and these he referred to as wholesome actions. The process that makes this happen is not a judgmental force doling out reward and punishment, he said, but is simply the natural law of cause and effect.

Throughout the decades following his awakening, Buddha frequently explained specific events in the lives of people he met by pointing to actions they had committed in previous lives. He asserted that these statements were not speculation or intuitive hunches, but were based on his own perception of the relationships connecting one life to another.

Confidence in the Buddha and the Dharma most often either

arises when people actually experience for themselves the validity of the Buddha's teachings by following the path he mapped out or when they learn about the life and qualities of the Buddha. Let us now take a brief look at his life.

Siddhārtha Buddha

In the life in which he attained full spiritual awakening, the person who came to be a Buddha was born as the son of a king, in the region that is now the border between India and Nepal. When prince Gautama Siddhārtha was born, wise men foretold that he was destined to become either a world monarch or, if he renounced worldly aspirations, an Awakened Being, that is, a Buddha. His father, intent on seeing his son become a great king, did everything in his power to make the prince thoroughly satisfied with palace life. The child grew into a handsome youth, excelling in all the skills and arts of royalty, and as a young man he married a lovely bride who soon bore him a son.

We could say that at this point he was moving smoothly along a success track leading to power, prosperity, and fame. But despite the luxurious life his father had provided for him, Siddhārtha, after having journeyed outside the palace on several occasions and truly recognized suffering for the first time, became acutely aware of the universal realities of aging, illness, and death. Whatever enchantment he may have felt for mundane enjoyments quickly vanished. On observing a wandering mendicant one day, he became inspired to seek the truth that liberates through a life devoted entirely to the spiritual quest. Quietly he slipped away from the palace and out of his princely role.

At this time India was home to many diverse philosophies, religious traditions, and meditative disciplines. Siddhārtha followed a wise course: he sought out one of the foremost masters of meditation who claimed to have experienced liberation. Siddhārtha, then in his late twenties, was trained by this sage. To the amazement and delight of his teacher, he swiftly attained extremely subtle stages of *samādhi*, or meditative absorption, in which one moves through states of ecstasy and beyond to formless realms of experience that transcend joy and sorrow.

When his mentor was convinced that his disciple had equaled his own realizations, he invited him to teach along with him. But with penetrating insight, Siddhārtha saw that the attainment he had reached provided only a respite from the persistent discontent of existence. The fundamental source of dissatisfaction and misery was not yet dispelled.

So Siddhārtha graciously declined his teacher's offer and sought out another contemplative who was even more adept at refining and stabilizing the mind. Under this one's guidance, Siddhārtha soon reached yet subtler degrees of concentration, equaling those of his new teacher; but these, too, he found ultimately unsatisfactory. In short, he had reached the pinnacle of the contemplative sciences of his time, at which India was possibly unsurpassed, and he was unsatisfied.

Feeling that there was nothing more to learn from the state-of-the-art techniques of samādhi, he explored another main avenue of spiritual practice, namely extreme asceticism. But six years after his departure from the palace, a period devoted to the most intense physical discipline and austerities, he concluded that this approach only weakened the body and mind, making him less fit to contemplate the nature of reality.

Siddhārtha then settled on a middle way between worldly life and extreme asceticism. With his health restored, it occurred to him to employ a vigorous, lucid state of samādhi as his instrument for investigating reality. With this quality of awareness, his attention gained great lucidity and stability, enabling him to analyze a subject with extraordinary clarity. Siddhārtha was now confident that he was on the threshold of the fulfillment of his yearning. As he sat down in meditation, he resolved not to rise until he was fully "awakened." Soon he was assailed by a host of forces intent on diverting him from his quest. Aggression, lust, and other afflictions rose up to overpower him, but he remained unmoved, and in the end they were vanquished.

During the first watch of the night prior to his enlightenment, Siddhārtha directed his refined awareness to the succession of former lives. He investigated these as far back as the previous cosmic eons, and he observed the specific circumstances of each birth, life, and death. From this realization, which contemplatives before him had also experienced to varying degrees, he gained profound insight into the fluctuating and insubstantial nature of cyclic existence. Attachment to the mundane concerns of a single lifetime appeared utterly futile.

In the second watch of the night, Siddhārtha explored the relationships between actions and their results from lifetime to lifetime. He saw that, in most cases, sentient beings are not capable of choosing their future rebirths; rather they are helplessly propelled from one existence to another by the force of previous actions. And with this realization great compassion for all living creatures arose within him.

During the third watch of the night, he thoroughly examined the truth of suffering, its source, the cessation of suffering and its causes, and the path leading to cessation. These came to be known as the Four Noble Truths. He also investigated the dependently related events that perpetuate the cycle of rebirth. He identified ignorance as the first link in this revolving sequence of events, and saw that overcoming attachment is instrumental in dispelling this root cause of dissatisfaction.

At dawn the final obscurations veiling Siddhārtha's mind were dispelled, and he experienced the full awakening of Buddhahood. He knew that never again would he be compelled to take rebirth; he was forever free from the cycle of existence and from the mental afflictions and obscurations that perpetuate that cycle.

Throughout the rest of his long life, the Buddha traveled around India as a simple mendicant, revealing the path of awakening to people in all walks of life, from paupers to kings. Among the first to be blessed by his enlightenment were his own father, former wife, and son. The grief they had experienced when he abandoned them years before was now immeasurably surpassed by the joys of spiritual realization to which he led them. It was out of compassion for all living beings that he first ventured forth on his spiritual quest, and his life following his awakening was unceasingly devoted to the welfare of the world.

WHAT IS ENLIGHTENMENT?

Within the Buddhist tradition there are different interpretations of the meaning of the Buddha's "omniscience." The most conservative of these asserts that wherever a Buddha's awareness is directed, the chosen object can be perceived without obstruction. Thus, when the Buddha sought the karmic cause of a current situation, the causal event immediately became apparent to his mind, even though it might have occurred many eons ago. A Buddha's vision is also unobstructed by material objects. There are many accounts from the Buddha's life that attest to these abilities.

The Buddha's ability to perceive the inclinations and backgrounds of individuals was also free of obstruction, and his compassion reached out to all creatures without discrimination. With an unimaginably limitless depth of kindness, he responded to the specific spiritual needs of sentient beings by revealing to them the aspect of Dharma that would bring them the greatest benefit.

At times he realized that a display of supernormal powers would inspire others to seek liberation, and with compassionate motivation he performed a variety of wondrous feats. But the Buddha's chief means of serving others was through teaching the Dharma, and this he did for more than four decades after his awakening.

Even his death, or final liberation, served as a teaching; it taught that even the body of a Buddha is subject to impermanence, so there is no benefit in clinging to this outer form.

The essence of the Buddha's message is contained in the Four Noble Truths. The first of these is the truth of suffering, and the Buddha admonished his followers to recognize it! At first glance it may seem odd that he should encourage us to do something that we already do. Who has not felt pain and discontent? But something deeper is meant here.

The Buddha declared that all our experiences of joy, indifference, and pain are unsatisfactory. Are not even our greatest mundane pleasures tainted with dissatisfaction? When these pleasures pass away are we not left with unfulfilled longing and discontent? But in spite of this, we tend to cling to the pleasures of life, ignoring their transient nature.

The Buddha encouraged us to overcome this refusal to confront reality. To fully realize the unsatisfactory nature of this life in cyclic existence can be a devastating experience. But it can also open the way to an authentic practice of Dharma, and this is why the Buddha emphasized the truth of suffering.

The suffering we must recognize includes not only the kind we experience at the loss of a loved one, or when we lose our job, for example, but also includes the more fundamental conditions of our human existence, namely, aging, sickness, and death. To think we will be released from suffering once this life is over is mere wishful thinking—from the Buddhist perspective there is too much evidence to the contrary.

One of my Tibetan teachers, the contemplative Gen Lamrimpa, spoke of his early reflections on death. As a young man he longingly wondered if death might simply mean the cessation of all experience. How comforting that would be: instant, effortless liberation from all life's woes! But he decided the matter was so important that it required thorough investigation. As a result of many years of study and meditation, he concluded that on both theoretical and empirical grounds the nihilistic view of death is untenable. Waiting around to die or hastening that event is no solution to the problem of suffering.

THE PATH

The Buddha offered no support to the view that we, as individuals or as a species, are naturally evolving toward liberation from lifetime to lifetime whether we try or not. The path of Dharma requires conscious, skillful effort. Without Dharma, each individual's continuum of awareness continues without end, moving from one dissatisfaction to the next. The Buddha was not content to reach states of awareness that bring mere temporary bliss or peace. He was seeking ultimate liberation from the cycle of existence. And this was his great discovery.

There are two Sanskrit words that have made their way into the English language, though often with their meanings somewhat misconstrued. The first of these is *samsāra*. Many people are familiar with this term, though it is frequently used quite loosely. Sometimes the whole universe is referred to as samsāra, but occasionally the word is used to refer more specifically to human civilization, or one's home city, job, or living conditions. To escape samsāra then in this context would mean to exit from the cosmos, to go out into the wilderness, or leave one's job, or home.

Although appealing, the truth is that samsāra, like so much unwanted baggage, will still accompany the traveler who "exits," for samsāra can be best understood as an inner condition of existence, not a place. Samsāra is the condition of being subject to the cycle of birth, aging, sickness, and death, the cycle of being propelled from one life to another by the force of one's own mental distortions and the actions conditioned by them.

Nirvāṇa, the second of these Sanskrit terms, means final liberation from that condition of samsaric existence. It does not mean one is annihilated, blown out like a light. With the attainment of nirvāṇa, one is no longer compelled to take birth by the force of mental distortions and tainted actions.

So one does not "go to" nirvāṇa; it is not a place, not heaven, nor is it nothingness. Instead, liberation, or the attainment of nirvāṇa, means a person is finally freed from the mental afflictions of confusion, attachment, and hatred. Fear and anxiety, pain and discontent are banished. According to Tibetan Buddhism, one may indeed continue to take birth, motivated by compassion for those who are bound in saṃsāra, but this act then becomes a matter of choice, an expression of freedom, not of bondage.

Disenchantment with saṃsāra, and the wish to attain nirvāṇa, occur after one reflects at length on the nature of suffering and cyclic existence. This is what is meant by cultivating a spirit of emergence. However, the attainment of nirvāṇa normally requires more than a single lifetime of spiritual practice. The task of overcoming all mental distortions, together with their latent impressions, is one that few of us are likely to complete in this life. Thus, in order to mature spiritually from this life to the next until liberation is won, it is essential to be reborn into circumstances conducive to Dharma practice. We can create such conditions for ourselves by avoiding unwholesome behavior, by devoting ourselves to the wholesome, and by dedicating our efforts to the attainment of liberation.

Meditating on the truth of suffering as it applies to ourselves is a means of cultivating a spirit of emergence. Meditating on the suffering of others leads to compassion. If our understanding of the nature of suffering is superficial, whatever compassion we feel for others may be little more than sentimentality: it arises when we see overt suffering, but as soon as that suffering is either pacified or forgotten, compassion vanishes. But as insight into the truth of suffering deepens, compassion may arise even toward those who are enjoying excellent health and prosperity. Our compassion embraces all beings who

41

are subject to mental afflictions, all those who, while striving for happiness, create the conditions for their own misery.

THE FOUNDATION OF JOY

Buddhism is sometimes accused of being a pessimistic world view, and it is true that many of the Buddhist teachings focus on the realities of impermanence and suffering. The Buddha even went so far as to declare that what ordinary beings regard as pleasure is merely another form of suffering. Why? Because, due to its transient nature pleasure must terminate, and when it does, we are ultimately left with dissatisfaction.

Is it true then that all experience in saṃsāra is pervaded by suffering? Are all mundane pleasures nothing more than a temporary decrease of suffering? Does mundane happiness not stem from an authentic source of joy?

Let's investigate these premises by examining something we normally consider to be pleasurable. If the stimulus for this enjoyment is joyful by nature, the pleasure derived from it should continue as long as the stimulus is applied; that is, it should never fade into boredom. Moreover, increasing the intensity or quantity of that stimulus should correspondingly increase the pleasure. Can we say this is true of such pleasures as eating, having sex, hoarding great sums of money, owning many possessions, going on frequent vacations, having children, being with friends?

None of these events invariably stimulate pleasure; they are unreliable. We can never count on them as sources of continuing happiness, and an increase in their quantity does not necessarily bring greater pleasure. In reality, joy does not have its source in any outer stimuli. It arises from the mind, and ultimate joy emerges from a mind that is free of suffering, distortion, and obscuration.

Another worthwhile experiment is to calm the mind temporarily, freeing it from the distraction of both pleasant and unpleasant stimuli. Mental stabilization has been cultivated by thousands of contemplatives over thousands of years, and the results of this inner calmness and clarity have been well documented: an unprecedented state of bliss arises from a profoundly stable and lucid mind. This event had already been thoroughly researched by generations of contemplatives at the time of the Buddha; and it was this kind of practice that at first seemed most promising to the young Siddhārtha when he set off on his quest for the state of nirvāṇa.

But as Siddhārtha found out for himself, meditative stabilization by itself yields only a temporary respite from suffering, for it does not eliminate the underlying causes of dissatisfaction. However, this practice does offer valuable insight into the origins of pleasure and pain and is a valuable aid on the path of Dharma.

5

THE ROOTS OF DISCONTENT

When the Buddha spoke of the need to recognize suffering, he was referring to a broad array of feelings ranging from a vague sense of malaise to overwhelming pain and grief. He was also referring to something even more fundamental: our state of being that makes us vulnerable to misery.

This leads to a very basic question: Why are we subject to suffering at all? Why is it that after having even the most satisfying and pleasurable experiences, we eventually return to a state of discontent? If, then, we can identify the sources of discontent, we might be able to reduce or even eliminate them. Also, when seeking the roots of discontent we are faced with another basic question: Are those roots to be found outside in our environment, or do they dwell within us? An experiment can be conducted that sheds light on this matter. Take a person who is in reasonably good physical and psychological health, and place him in solitude. Make sure the room is comfortable and clean, and that all physical needs such as food and personal hygiene, are adequately met. The only entertainment to be allowed this person is his own body, mind, and the quiescent environment.

What happens to this person as the days, weeks, and months pass in isolation? In most cases the individual rapidly becomes bored and restless, and deepening unhappiness sets in. Although his mind is not subjected to any painful stimuli from the environment, nevertheless it becomes increasingly turbulent and distressed. He becomes frustrated by dwelling on the many things he wants but cannot have, and innocuous events such as minor noises and imperfections in the food that is served result in intense irritation.

Buddhism would say that these emotional outbursts cannot really be attributed to insignificant outer irritations; nor do they essentially stem from relative sensory deprivation. Rather, they originate from the mind's imbalance, which is now unmasked by the absence of outer distractions.

It is no wonder solitary confinement is a severe form of punishment in prisons. Isolated from the distractions of ordinary prison life, the prisoner is subjected to the unmitigated tortures of his own mind. Thus, the Buddha declared:

> The mind that has perverted aims
> Causes one greater misery
> Than the hater [does] the hated,
> Than enemies do enemies.[5]

Clearly a prison cell is not the neutral environment suggested in the above experiment. But contemplatives on long retreats often subject themselves to conditions very similar to those described here.

Drawing from my own and others' experience in lengthy retreats, I have found that during the early stages of isolation, the mind tends to become filled with turbulent thoughts and emotions. If the retreatant blames his unhappiness on his environment—upon external personal or impersonal stimuli—he remains trapped by it. Frustration, resentment, and rage mount in a crescendo of emotional agony that abates only with his release from solitude and a change of environment.

On the other hand, if the solitary contemplative recognizes that the true source of distress lies in is his own mind, he opens the door to freedom from his mental afflictions. Under skillful guidance, and with a wholesome motivation, he may alleviate these afflictions and tap the fathomless source of goodness and joy that lies in the innermost depths of his mind. As this occurs, he begins to experience an unprecedented state of well-being that arises, not from outer pleasurable stimuli, but from a harmonious mind. Thus, the Buddha declared:

> The mind that has perfected aims
> Brings happiness to oneself.
> Fathers, mothers, and other friends
> Do not cause such happiness as that.[6]

In the course of a day, the distortions of our minds occasionally erupt with hostility toward disagreeable events, and with agitated grasping desire toward the agreeable. The conceptual turmoil and emotional unrest that manifest so virulently when one is in solitude are only thinly veiled in the course of a socially active life. So it is certainly within the mental domain of these afflictions that we must search, if we want to find the source of our discontent.

As mentioned before, the task of identifying the full extent of suffering and its origins, and forever freeing ourselves from them, is considered the fundamental challenge in Buddhism. We are concerned here with more than simply finding greater well-being in this life: we wish to utterly uproot the sources of discontent in this and all future existences.

The Buddha declared that we are thrown into conditioned existence by two things: mental distortions and the actions influenced by them. These actions place impressions upon our mindstreams, which in turn generate future rebirths. For these mindstream impressions to influence our rebirths, they must be stimulated by mental distortions such as attachment. If a person were to have no mental distortions to stimulate them, they would remain latently inactive. Thus, even if one had a tremendous store of unwholesome imprints upon one's mind, and one subsequently freed the mind of all distortions, those imprints could not produce karmic results.

Conversely, let us take the hypothetical case of a person whose mindstream is free of karmic impressions but is still subject to distortions. Because of these distortions the person is compelled to act in ways that would cause his mindstream to accumulate karma very rapidly, and of course those imprints would be catalyzed by the mental distortions. For these reasons it is more crucial to identify and dispel those distortions than their resultant karmic imprints. Between the two sources of suffering—mental distortions and tainted actions—the former are more essential.

In Buddhism the fundamental afflictions of the mind are known as the three poisons: ignorance, hatred, and attachment. Among these, ignorance is the root distortion from which hatred and attachment stem. All other mental afflictions, such as jealousy and pride, derive from these three poisons.

REASON AND FAITH

The Buddha's teachings are generally of two types. The first focuses on issues we can presently test and possibly confirm with our own powers of perception and logic. To a large extent the subject of suffering and its origins, and the nature of consciousness and its continuity from life to life, fall into this category. It is conceivable that these Buddhist assertions could be disproved by empirical experiment or logic, just as they can be verified by those means. Concerning this class of teachings the Buddha counseled his followers:

> O monks, just as a goldsmith tests his gold
> By melting, cutting, and rubbing,
> Sages accept my teachings after full examination,
> And not just out of devotion [to me].[7]

By examining the Buddhist teachings on the nature of consciousness, and the evidence supporting the theory of transmigration, we may decide this theory is meaningful. But as soon as we move on to further questions, such as the precise nature of the relationships between our successive lives, we enter a domain that is beyond our ken. Here we must either resort to faith or stop our quest. Most likely the Buddha was referring especially to this aspect of his teachings when he declared:

> Angry or agitated minds,
> Or minds without faith, are unable
> To comprehend all the holy doctrine
> Which the completed Buddha taught.[8]

The fragmentation between faith and reason in our Western world view has wrought much harm in our society. One way it does this is by ignoring the crucial role of faith in philosophy and science. Confidence, conviction, and enthusiasm in the search for understanding in all fields rest upon faith of some sort, regardless of the specific nature of one's quest. In Buddhism, both faith and reason are crucial as the Buddha himself asserted:

> The wise take faith and intelligence
> For their security in life;
> These are their finest wealth.
> That other wealth is just commonplace.[9]

Many people have found that a close scrutiny of many of the Buddha's teachings, relying on experience and intelligence, gives rise to deepening faith in the authenticity of the Buddha's awakening. It is also certainly true that sincere faith—not to be confused with dogmatic belief—enhances and empowers understanding and wisdom. This expresses itself in a deep confidence in the Buddha and his Dharma, and it allows us to be receptive to fresh ideas and perspectives. We regard the Dharma with a sense of humility that is not debasing, but rather affirms and exalts our own intuitive wisdom. Such faith is the indispensable fertile ground of spiritual growth and awakening.

MENTAL DISTORTIONS

With this in mind, let us seek a more thorough theoretical understanding of mental distortions. In our lives most of us already know a great deal about these distortions; we are no strangers to ignorance, hatred, and attachment. Since we are afflicted by these tendencies every day of our lives, it makes sense to have more than a casual interest in them. Although we have often experienced mental distortions and suffering, we may not have examined closely enough the relationship between them.

All of us have frequently felt frustration, discontent, and pain of many varieties, but how have we responded to them? The most common response to suffering is to blame it on something external. The search for the sources of suffering is not a fresh idea suggested by the Buddha. We do it all the time, and we often think we have identified the true cause of our dissatisfaction: "The reason I'm unhappy is due to something out there." Is it not true that when we feel happy, we tend to attribute this, also, to external circumstances?

The essential truth of suffering is that neither individual nor social problems are due chiefly to external conditions. Those influences may be very important at times, but our efforts to solve both types of problems by focusing on outer conditions alone are bound to be largely ineffective and superficial. Instead, contemplative insight into the depths of human nature is essential to relieving suffering on a global level; and compassionate concern for others can deepen one's own introspective wisdom.

According to the Buddha, the essential source of all suffering, fear, and conflict is ignorance. However, in the case of physical pain, for example from a broken leg, the causal role of ignorance is not at all evident. Moreover, when we empathize with someone else's sorrow we suffer with them, and the source of our own grief seems to be compassion, not ignorance.

Buddhism speaks of two types of ignorance that act as causes of suffering. The first is a state of unknowing, specifically an absence of clear awareness. In each moment of our lives countless psycho-physiological events take place. Physical sensations arise and vanish throughout the body, physical and mental feelings of pleasure, pain, and indifference occur, and sensory and mental forms of conscious-ness arise in a constant state of flux, joined with a wide array of thoughts, inclinations, discriminations, and so forth.

People who cultivate mindfulness in meditation are often taken aback by the sheer quantity of mental events they discover in each moment, events they were unaware of until they tried to still their minds. In meditation the currents of conceptualization, for instance, are found to be multiple, swift, turbulent, and for the most part, incessant. The mind is revealed as a gushing well of compulsive ideation: thoughts, recollections, associations, fantasies, desires, and emotions are spewed forth from an apparently inexhaustible source. A meditator will find himself caught in the congestion of mental rush-hour traffic, even though he has gone into seclusion to meditate.

All these mental events fluctuate with each moment as they arise and pass away, conditioned by events in the body and the environment, as well as by previous thoughts and emotions. In the meantime, tactile sensations occur in the body, together with their associated feelings; the other sensory faculties of seeing, hearing, smelling, and tasting operate with varying degrees of dominance.

In our day-to-day states of unclear awareness, we do not recog-nize the arising of these events moment by moment; we do not see their subtle and complex interrelationships, nor do we comprehend their nature or how they pass from existence. In short, our aware-ness of being alive in the world is very hazy.

In addition to this lack of clear awareness of the body, mind, and environment, there is a more dynamic form of ignorance that exerts itself. This ignorance, the second type, does not merely overlook the nature of these events, it actively misconstrues them. Lacking a clear perception of the origin of thoughts, for example, this ignorance imputes upon them the notion that "I am thinking these thoughts." Similarly, it identifies mental and physical events as "mine"; and not seeing the interrelationships among them, it imputes, "I am in control of them." The body, consciousness, emotions, thoughts—all of these are regarded by ignorance as "my possessions."

And who is this "I" that ignorance designates as the master of the body and mind? If this "I" could speak, it would say something like this: "I am the person in charge; my body and mind act according to my will; I am self-sufficient and exist among the transitory events of my body and mind, and I coordinate them into a meaningful whole. Although I, too, am subject to change, my own identity is more stable and enduring than the psycho-physical events that I see as mine. For I have a past and I will have a future."

It is not particularly helpful to accept this explanation of the two types of ignorance, passive unknowing and active misconstruing, simply as a matter of Buddhist doctrine. Since our own suffering is a matter of vital concern to each of us, its origin deserves careful scrutiny, so we really know where it comes from. The Buddha encouraged each of us to check this out for ourselves. Do we experience the first type of ignorance which springs from a lack of mindfulness? Do we gloss over the subtleties of psycho-physical events by designating all of them as "mine"? Do we conceive of ourselves as the kind of personal identity described above?

Buddhism asserts that this false sense of "I" is inborn. We do not acquire it from our environment nor do we learn it from others; we are born with it. In the process of being educated, we may develop additional rationales for the existence of this "I"; and we may construct elaborate theories based on the assumption of its existence. In this way, inborn ignorance defends itself with acquired ignorance. Here is a premise we can test with our own experience.

The Buddha declared that the sense of oneself as a self-sufficient, substantial "I" which is in charge of the body and mind, is a delusion. The notion of a self-existent personal identity is inborn, but it is also ignorant and acts as a source of suffering. This "I" that is so conceived does not exist at all. It is useful, however, to distinguish between the mental process of misconceiving the "I," and the self-sufficient "I" itself that is so imagined. The false sense of "I" does exist and exerts a strong influence on our other mental functions and on the course of our lives, while the fictitious "I" itself does nothing, because it does not exist at all.

The false notion of selfhood gives rise to a feeling of separateness from everyone else, and from this follows the affliction of attachment. This mental distortion grasps at inner and outer attractive objects, craves them and becomes absorbed in them, so that it is difficult to disengage the attention from them. Attachment filters out disagreeable qualities from our awareness of the craved object, and it accentuates and embellishes the agreeable qualities.

A person may also experience attachment toward his own personal appearance. In this case, his features, whatever they may be, are seen as special and desirable, and the chief reason for their attractiveness is that they are regarded as his. So again there arises attachment to "me" and "mine": "my" emotions, intelligence, views, body, spouse, children, friends, reputation, possessions, and environment. In all of these cases, attachment screens out awareness of the negative qualities of the object, and enhances awareness of the desirable ones.

In general, the less supportive an object appears to one's own well-being, the less attached one is to it. There are many things that seem irrelevant to one's welfare, and the common reaction toward these is indifference. But when things appear hostile to one's well-being, the mental affliction of hatred arises. Hatred focuses on suffering and things that seem to cause pain, including sentient beings and inanimate agents of pain; and it aggressively seeks ways to retaliate against them. Like attachment, it distorts our awareness of reality, but in the opposite direction: it filters out the agreeable and enhances the disagreeable.

The Buddha asserted that the three mental afflictions of ignorance, hatred, and attachment are the roots of all suffering. This is a monumental statement that is comparable to the greatest theories of physical science. Isaac Newton, for example, took into account the great variety of motions in nature—from the straight movement of a falling apple to the revolutions of the moon around the earth—and explained them all in three simple laws. Similarly, a vast array of natural events can be understood and predicted using the single, unifying principle of the conservation of mass-energy. The Buddha was concerned chiefly not with physical laws but with the natural laws of sentient existence. Having deeply explored the nature of suffering and its origin, the Buddha concluded that the roots of all discontent are to be found in the mind, specifically in the three poisons that control the mind. This idea serves as a vast, unifying principle of experience whose validity we can test for ourselves.

Let us take a look at a few derivative mental distortions that stem from the three poisons. Pride is a mental factor based on a distorted view of the self, that focuses on qualities—good or bad, high or low—with a sense of conceit and superiority. With this sense of pride we feel superior to others due to a certain quality— virtue, intelligence, or beauty—that we each consider to be inherently "ours." Pride, while originating from ignorance, also reinforces the false sense of ego, exalting it as superior to other egos.

Another derivative affliction is doubt about such issues as the truth of suffering, its source, its cessation, and the path to that cessation. It is a form of skepticism, not to be confused with critical inquiry.

When we study Buddhism with a true thirst for greater understanding, misgivings and uncertainties are bound to arise. With this motivation we can critically ponder the Buddhist teachings, test them with our experience, and try to clear up uncertainties by questioning competent teachers. Western students of Buddhism are particularly known for this approach. Most Tibetan Lamas I know who have taught in the West are first somewhat surprised, then quickly become delighted, by the penetrating way with which Westerners question them. One Lama, after lecturing on Buddhism in the United States for almost two years, spent several days teaching a small group of devout Tibetans living in this country. When I spoke with him shortly afterward, I asked him how it went. He replied, "I think it went pretty well, but I don't really know what they learned, for they didn't ask a single question!"

While faith is essential for the cultivation of profound understanding, its benefits are curtailed when it is combined with a complacent, unquestioning attitude. For example, when we first encounter the Buddhist theory of transmigration, our understanding is bound to be seriously flawed and incomplete. If our initial response is to accept this doctrine uncritically, then our understanding will not mature, and we will be stuck with ill-formed and possibly misleading beliefs. It is much better to press ahead with a zeal for comprehending reality, using Buddhist teachings as a malleable tool in our quest for truth.

Doubt in the sense of wavering skepticism, which paralyzes the seeker, is quite another matter, and it can be at least as debilitating as blind faith. Instead of helping a seeker forge ahead on the path of understanding, this kind of doubt will cause him to meander about among various possibilities, without thoroughly exploring any of them.

The mental affliction of doubt may affect practice as well as theory. For instance, one may decide to engage in a certain type of meditation. But after a couple of weeks, once the novelty has worn off, one begins to wonder, "Should I continue with this practice or try out that other one that I heard about? I might get better results with that one, since I'm not really sure this one is right for me."

This wavering attitude can lead a practitioner to try out a wide range of methods without gaining deep benefit from any of them. Doubt may also turn on one's own ability for practice and cause us to think, "This seems to be a valuable method, but maybe it's too advanced for me. After all, I'm just a beginner, and I don't seem to have much of a knack for meditation anyway. Maybe I should tackle something else, or just not bother at all." Tibetans liken these forms of vacillation to trying to insert a frayed thread through the eye of a needle: as soon as one strand of the thread goes through, the other strands veer off in other directions, and the job never gets done.

Another derivative mental distortion is a view that grasps at extremes. It is based on the assumption that the "I" exists as a self-sufficient controller of "my" body and mind, and it is concerned with the questions: "What will become of me? When I die, will I be annihilated, or will I continue to exist in some way?" In fact, neither of these alternatives is true, for the notion of self that underlies the questions is false. Such an autonomous "I" will neither be destroyed nor will it persist beyond death; for it never existed in the first place.

FREE WILL

In the face of the Buddhist assertion that I do not exist as an independent entity that controls my body and mind, this question is bound to arise: "Do I not then have free will?" To grapple with this question I must understand all the components of the question, that is, the meaning of free will, of "I," and the sense in which this "I" might possess such a will.

Will involves intention and the decision-making process. What does it mean for it to be free? Does free will imply that intentions occur autonomously, without being influenced by earlier conditions or outer circumstances? This interpretation would be silly, for my decisions would then have nothing to do with my past or my present environment. A more meaningful interpretation of free will maintains that my intentions are influenced by past and present conditions, but they are not wholly determined by them. Choices are freely made by me, using my own powers of judgment, which have been conditioned by my past.

Now, what is the nature of this "I" that many people assert has free will? If Buddhism is right, and I do not exist as an independent entity absolutely in charge of my body and mind—including my will—then the notion of my having free will becomes very problematic.

Regardless of how I may exist, other questions arise: "To what extent am I free to choose how I respond to situations? For instance, if someone insults me, do I have the freedom to respond with equanimity or friendliness and understanding? Do I have the freedom to choose not to be upset? More generally, am I free to decide to feel or not feel jealousy, attachment, and anger? Can I freely decide not to have a conceptually and emotionally turbulent mind?" Each of us can answer these questions of freedom for ourselves, and most of us will probably respond immediately that we lack such freedom. In this context, the question of free will can be settled experientially, without elaborate philosophical speculation.

Most of us find our minds are dominated by mental distortions, and in this important sense our intentions and decisions are not free. Can we ever make choices free of the influences of ignorance, hatred, and desire? The Buddha responded that we have this potential, and the practices that he taught are designed to lead us to such liberation. "But," we might ask, "what about the other kind of free will? Even when my mind is not dominated by a mental distortion, do I then make my choices freely? In other words, do I stand apart from even wholesome mental influences, such as wisdom and compassion, in exerting free will?" To answer this question to our own satisfaction, I believe we must have profound, experiential insight into the manner in which we do exist. Without that, any response that either asserts or denies the existence of free will must be incomplete and possibly misleading.

THE NATURE AND EFFECTS OF MENTAL DISTORTIONS

In the preceding discussion we examined various primary and secondary mental distortions, and there are many others that have not been mentioned. What do they all have in common? What are the criteria for designating a mental event as a distortion? The Sanskrit term that I have translated as distortion is *kleśa*, which literally means affliction. Ignorance, hatred, attachment, and their derivatives are kleśas, and all bring us distress and dissatisfaction. They are the essential causes of all unwholesome behavior and of suffering. However, I must add that mental and physical suffering themselves are not regarded as kleśas. In fact, suffering may arise together with a wholesome state of mind, such as compassion.

Existentially, kleśas afflict us by disturbing the harmony and equilibrium of our minds. Cognitively, they distort our awareness of reality. Because of this dual aspect, I have translated this term as both *mental affliction* and *distortion*. It is crucial to gain a clear, theoretical understanding of the nature of kleśas in general, and of specific primary and secondary afflictions in particular, so that we can begin to identify them and explore their nature in daily life.

The fundamental affliction is ignorance, and the fundamental antidote to this affliction is insight. So the task before us is to move away from the tendency to ignore or repress mental distortions and instead develop insight into their nature and functioning.

In order to ascertain these mental events, it is essential to cease identifying with them. At the beginning it is advisable simply to observe them, examining the way they arise in relation to previous events. One inspects them carefully, clearly distinguishing them from other mental processes that are not distortions, and observes the effects they produce in one's own being. Finally, one notes the manner in which they vanish from consciousness.

When mental distortions arise without being watched by discriminating alertness, those distortions are suffused with confusion. When anger arises, for example, we often unconsciously identify with it, and express this by thinking, "I am angry" or "I hate this!" By this process of identification we create a self-image of ourselves as hot-tempered, greedy, confused, anxious, jealous, and so on.

Such a sense of personal identity is only partially, conventionally true, and it tends to cloud the actual nature of mental distortions. None of these mental afflictions is the "I," any more than cancer or tuberculosis is the "I." They are sources of distress from which we can be liberated. Although patterns of these distortions may be deeply ingrained in our mental behavior, they are not innate qualities of our minds.

We can test the Buddhist hypothesis that all suffering stems from mental distortions, and the experiment can start as soon as we experience unhappiness of any sort. As soon as we realize unhappiness has arisen, we can see if it stems from any identifiable mental distortion. Normally we blame our unhappiness on some external event, but the fallacy of this response becomes evident when we witness someone else responding to the same event without unhappiness.

While investigating the origins of unhappiness in this way, we may find occasions when mental distortions do not seem to play a role. We may feel distress at the misfortune of others and sorrow may appear to arise from intelligent concern and compassion. Indeed, it is true that if we did not care about other living creatures we would not experience such dismay. But for the time being, the compassion we feel is bound to be accompanied by distress. As our insight deepens, however, we find that the true source of such distress is not compassion, but subtle forms of attachment and ignorance that arise in relation to it.

The same can be said of physical pain. A person who has gained freedom from mental distortions through the cultivation of profound insight may still feel pain. It is not as if the body has received a general anesthetic. But the experience of pain is very different due to his ability to witness pain as a stream of events that may or may not need a response. The torment of physical suffering is due to ignorance and attachment, particularly related to the conception that "this is my body."

Mental distortions have afflicted us throughout our lives and for innumerable lifetimes in the past; and if we do not effectively use antidotes against them, they will persist indefinitely. We are accustomed to identifying and opposing outer enemies who have obstructed our well-being. But all the while we continue to suffer due to our failure to recognize and counter our true enemies—mental distortions. How do we get rid of them?

Buddhism suggests a radical response to mental afflictions: do not learn to cope with them; dispel them forever! For eons they have brought incalculable harm upon our mindstreams and consequently upon the world around us. The true culprits must be recognized, and we can begin by ceasing to identify with them. If we truly realize that we are victims of our own mental afflictions, we can stop condemning ourselves for our faults and shortcomings. We can sow the seeds of compassion for ourselves, and in so doing we can open the way to empathizing with others who are similarly afflicted.

Finally, let us end with an analogy. Imagine walking along a sidewalk with your arms full of groceries, and someone roughly bumps into you so that you fall and your groceries are strewn over the ground. As you rise up from the puddle of broken eggs and tomato juice, you are ready to shout out, "You idiot! What's wrong with you? Are you blind?" But just before you can catch your breath to speak, you see that the person who bumped you is actually blind. He, too, is sprawled in the spilled groceries, and your anger vanishes in an instant, to be replaced by sympathetic concern: "Are you hurt? Can I help you up?"

Our situation is like that. When we clearly realize that the source of disharmony and misery in the world is ignorance, we can open the door of wisdom and compassion. Then we are in a position to heal ourselves and others.

6

THE FRUITS OF OUR LABORS

Let us now return to the important question: If personal experience continues after death, what is the relationship between our behavior in this life and our experiences in future existences?

As we seek answers to this question, most of us must rely on someone else's knowledge, for neither our present experience nor our reasoning faculties alone are sufficient for the task. The following discussion is thoroughly based on the experience of the Buddha and later contemplatives.

In the West, most people already rely on information they cannot verify empirically or logically. Most scientific knowledge, for instance, is accepted by the general public without their fully understanding the empirical and theoretical basis of such knowledge. Even within the scientific community, with its high degree of specialization, chemists, for example, must rely upon prior discoveries in physics they cannot verify for themselves.

Such trust, when it is well-founded, is based on a tradition of critical inquiry: "What is the empirical evidence to support the theory? Was the research leading to it conducted reliably?" If the method of research is faulty, any resultant theory can be dismissed.

The following Buddhist description of the nature of actions and their results will lead us into alleged realms of experience that will likely stretch our imaginations and credulity. The Buddha declared that he observed the relationships that exist from one life to another, and he explained to others how he was able to make these observations.

Unlike religious prophets, he did not acquire his knowledge through divine revelation; unlike philosophers, he did not formulate his theories by logical analysis and speculation; and unlike scientists, he did not conduct his research with technological instruments. His sole research instrument was his own mind, finely honed by sophisticated contemplative discipline.

If our trust in his findings is to be based on critical inquiry, we must be persuaded the path leading to his spiritual awakening was authentic. We have several options to establish such authenticity. We can investigate this path theoretically, and we can also examine the findings of later contemplatives who became far advanced in the disciplines the Buddha set forth. Finally, and most important of all, we can enter into that discipline ourselves and make our own empirical discoveries.

If the Buddhist methods of contemplative research are reliable, can we conclude that the theories based upon them are necessarily true? Do they uniquely depict reality as it is? In grappling with this problem, we run into the same situation that is encountered in science: multiple theories may equally account for the same body of empirical evidence. Both Buddhist theories of actions and their results, and the theories of natural science, make intelligible a wide range of natural phenomena; and they allow us to view these events in ways that are highly useful. Neither set of theories need be regarded as true in the sense of describing or explaining some independent, objective reality; but both can be meaningful by presenting us with coherent and useful models of events in relation to human experience.

THE NATURE OF KARMA

The meaning of the term *karma* is action, and it refers specifically to intention. Intention is a mental factor that directs one's awareness to a given object or to a given activity. In Buddhism we can speak both of intention itself, and of intended action. While the former refers to a mental event, the latter refers chiefly to intentional physical and verbal behavior. Whenever we engage in intentional activities of the body, speech, and mind, whether wholesome or unwholesome, impressions are placed upon our mindstreams. These are like seeds or potencies, and are also termed *karma*. In certain situations these seeds act as *propulsive karma*. This karma is imprinted upon the subtle mindstream that carries on after death, and when it is stimulated by an appropriate catalyst, it propels one into another rebirth. The *fully ripened fruit* of this karma refers to the type of life-form that one takes, be it human or otherwise.

The *karmic results accordant with their causes* are of two types: behavioral and environmental. Behavioral results refer to patterns created in one life that carry over into the next. These include habitual ways of responding to life circumstances, for example with attachment, hostility, equanimity, or anxiety. Likewise, if we cultivate a great capacity for generosity, for music or mathematics, or for meditation, these behavioral causes will give rise to similar propensities in future lives; and they can be accentuated from life to life and become more and more developed. This aspect of karma accounts for the innate generosity of some children, for child prodigies in such fields as music and mathematics, and for the extraordinary abilities of some Tibetan *tulkus,* or incarnated spiritual masters. It also accounts for the unwholesome qualities and behavior that some children display from infancy.

Environmental results of karma follow the principle that what we put out into the world comes back to us. For example, if we have lived a generous life, in future lives we will be the recipient of others' generosity and will easily acquire food, clothing, and the like. The karmic results of killing, on the other hand, would be taking rebirth in a hostile environment, succumbing to serious illness, and possibly being killed. We reap what we have sown.

When a human dies and is propelled into another rebirth, it is not the former human being who dwells in the new body. This is an important point to remember, especially when considering the case of someone taking a nonhuman rebirth. Our present sense of self-hood is strongly identified with our human body and human mentality, which functions in dependence on the brain. But in the death process, the human sensory, conceptual, and emotional faculties shut down as the body loses its ability to support them. Thus, says Buddhism, the subtle mindstream that departs at death is not a human consciousness, and the "I" that was designated on our present body and mind vanishes. This continuum of awareness is now able to conjoin with another human organism or with a nonhuman life-form.

Let us look at the realms of experience where rebirth might take place. Generally speaking, there are three dimensions of existence that had been discovered by contemplatives before the time of the Buddha. The first of these is the one we are most familiar with called the *sensual* or *desire realm*. Here sentient beings generally experience strong desire for sensory objects, and human existence is included in this dimension of experience.

A more subtle dimension is called the *subtle material* or *form realm*. Sensory experience does exist in this dimension, but gross materiality is absent, as is sensual desire. The beings who dwell here are called *devas*, loosely translated as "gods." It is possible for humans to experience this experiential dimension by refining their awareness through the cultivation of high degrees of mental stability and clarity. It was this type of contemplative discipline in samādhi, or concentration, that Gautama first practiced when he set out on his spiritual quest. If, as a human being, one attains states of mental stabilization belonging to the subtle material realm, at death one may well be reborn as a deva in that realm. It is only through entering such meditative states that one acquires the karma to be reborn there.

By achieving even more refined states of samādhi, it is possible to gain access to a yet subtler dimension known as the *immaterial* or *formless realm*. This is the only means for taking rebirth there as a formless deva.

At the time of the Buddha, many Indian contemplatives regarded these states of samādhi as ultimate liberation from the cycle of existence. But the Buddha saw that the formless beings who dwell in this immaterial realm are mortal, despite the fact that their life spans may extend over numerous cosmic eons. Although such beings are undisturbed by the destruction of the material cosmos, the karma that propelled them into that existence is eventually exhausted, and they must return to the sensual realm. While mental distortions are suppressed in the subtle material and immaterial realms, they are not uprooted; and when those beings return to the sensual realm, those distortions manifest again as vigorously as ever.

It is important to recognize that the sensual, subtle material and immaterial dimensions are all realms of experience. They are interpenetrating and are not spatially separate. Thus, while seated on his meditation cushion, a contemplative's mind first experiences the sensual realm. Then, as he enters deeper states of samādhi, his mind, without moving elsewhere, may enter the other two realms. Similarly, the devas who inhabit the subtler realms may be said to exist amidst us humans, but on different "frequencies" of being.

According to Buddhist teachings, six types of sentient beings inhabit the three realms of existence, and we may be reborn into any of them. I have already mentioned devas, some of whom are found in the sensual realm. Here they appear in bodies of light, endowed with celestial beauty and superhuman powers of clairvoyance, and other psychic abilities. For the duration of their long lives they enjoy extraordinary sensual delights, but eventually they perish and with great dismay they must leave all these pleasures behind. Some devas are benevolently inclined toward human beings and can be called upon for assistance. This was common practice in Tibet, where certain devas were consulted through the medium of oracles. Even now, the Tibetan government in exile in northern India consults its own Nechung Oracle for matters of national importance.

Another class of superhuman beings, sometimes classified with the devas, are called *asuras*. They, too, have extraordinary powers, though not equal to the devas; and because of their inferior status they are consumed by jealousy. They are warlike beings, and their lives are focused on battling the devas, despite the fact that the asuras invariably lose.

⤴ The third class of sentient beings, namely humans, are said to have the widest potential range of experience of any beings in the universe. As humans, we can experience unbearable agony or inexpressible bliss; we may be intellectually retarded or brilliant; our behavior may range from the demonic to the saintly; and in meditation we may gain access to all three realms of existence. Most important, human existence offers the opportunity to attain nirvāṇa and the perfect spiritual awakening of a Buddha. Because of this capacity, human existence is regarded as the best for spiritual growth.

Only wholesome propulsive karma results in existence as a deva, asura, or a human. The other three classes of existence result from unwholesome propulsive karma.

The first of these is rebirth as an animal. The unwholesome behavior that causes an animal rebirth tends to be dominated by ignorance and confusion. If a human being leads a brutish life, the human physiological basis of his mind is left behind at death, and his mindstream conjoins with the body of a newly conceived animal.

If the propulsive karma is largely dominated by lust and desire, rebirth as a *preta* may ensue. Pretas are a diverse class of spirits, some malevolent and some not, which are all consumed with insatiated desire. While dwelling amongst humans, a preta's perception of reality is very different from ours. The Buddhist writings illustrate this as follows: If a deva, a human, and a preta look at a single vessel of liquid, the deva perceives the liquid as celestial elixir, the human sees it as water, and the preta views it as pus or some other foul substance. It is not uncommon for pretas to influence human affairs, sometimes through possession. Although they usually can perceive humans, they are only infrequently seen by us.

The most dismal of the three unfortunate realms of existence is that of the *nārakas*. The propulsive karma that leads to rebirth as a nāraka is often dominated by hatred, and the beings in this realm suffer extreme torment. The Buddha's descriptions of the various naraka realms are vividly and gruesomely reminiscent of Dante's descriptions of hell.

Because of the apparent similarities between certain Christian concepts of hell, it is especially important for Westerners to note important differences between the Buddhist and Christian views. According to Buddhism, existence as a nāraka is finite, ending as soon as the causal propulsive karma is exhausted. Moreover, the specific naraka realm that one experiences does not exist prior to one's appearance in it; its creation is simultaneous with one's "birth" in it, and it vanishes as soon as the inhabitant's karma is exhausted. (The same is equally true of existence as a deva.) Finally, the painful experiences of the nārakas are not inflicted upon them as punishment by anyone; their suffering is simply the natural result of their own previous actions.

As human beings we are capable of actions that lead to any of the six realms of existence. The force of the resultant propulsive karma is directed by our desires. If we wish to be reborn in any of the three favorable realms of existence, we must devote ourselves to wholesome behavior. If we wish our wholesome karma to lead to human rebirth, this will likely be its result. If we are interested in birth as a deva or as an asura, we can direct our wholesome energies that way. However, if our lives are largely dominated by unwholesome behavior, the most probable result will be rebirth in one of the three unfavorable realms. The specific realm to which we migrate will depend upon the nature and intensity of our unwholesome actions.

THE PROCESS OF DEATH

In terms of karma, there are three conditions that lead to death. The first is the simple exhaustion of the propulsive karma that caused one's present life. Second, one may use up the accumulated merit from previous altruistic actions, which will leave one without the necessities for survival: food, clothing, lodging and, at times, medicine.

The key to this is the fact that it is possible to lead an ethical life without going out of one's way to be of service to others. The propulsive karma from ethical behavior leads to favorable rebirth, but it may be conjoined with only a little merit. So, for example, if one leads a moral but ungenerous life, this could lead to rebirth as a human who dies of starvation. If one's merit is exhausted—even if one's life-force remains—death will occur because one lacks the means of survival.

A third cause of death is meeting with fatal circumstances. This could be an automobile accident, illness, or war, or it could be self-inflicted as in the case of suicide. As a result of previous unwholesome karma, death may occur even though one's life-force and merit are not yet used up.

One's state of mind just prior to death strongly influences one's experiences thereafter. According to the Buddhist teachings, if one dies with a wholesome mind, one has the sense of moving from darkness to light, and one may experience wonderful, dream-like visions. The transition of death tends to be smooth, with little pain or discomfort. The entire death process may be peaceful and untroubled—nothing to fear or dread.

If one dies with an unwholesome state of mind, especially one dominated by anger, one feels that one is moving from light to darkness. Unpleasant, possibly frightening apparitions are seen, and the pain of death may be intense. Finally, if one's state of mind just prior to death is neutral, the experience of death tends to be bland, with little or no experience of pleasure or pain.

The state of mind at death is, of course, largely determined by one's behavior throughout the course of one's life. If one's mind is predominantly unwholesome during the years preceding death, it is unlikely that a wholesome attitude will arise when one faces death. We are creatures of habit, and it is difficult to choose virtuous thoughts in a crisis situation, especially if we have built our lives on a foundation of unwholesomeness. So if we want to forecast the condition of our minds at death, we can do so by examining our thoughts and emotions from day to day.

Right now we are sowing the seeds of the kind of death we will experience. Our mental habits throughout life largely determine the quality of our experience of death; this strongly influences the nature of the intermediate state following death; and that period leads directly to our next rebirth.

The Buddha showed how to subdue mental distortions and cultivate wholesome qualities of mind. But simply calling oneself a Buddhist is no guarantee one will experience a favorable rebirth; nor do non-Buddhists necessarily fall to unfavorable rebirths. In terms of karma, the crucial issue is the moral quality of one's life, not the specific metaphysical doctrine that one adopts.

During the initial stages of the death process, the mind may be wholesome, unwholesome, or neutral. As the death process continues, feelings of pleasure and pain and all conceptualization vanish, and one enters a very subtle state of consciousness. After this phase, conceptualization reasserts itself out of the force of habituation. At this point one has no sense of having a body, and when one finds that there is nothing to grasp onto, suddenly the fear arises: "I shall cease to exist!" This leads to desire for a body, which in turn thrusts one into the *bardo*, or intermediate state between death and rebirth.

THE INTERMEDIATE STATE

As we mentioned earlier, the process of dying is similar to the process of falling asleep; the intermediate state can be likened to dreaming; and rebirth, or conception, is analogous to waking up.

For now let us focus on the similarities between the intermediate state and dreaming. While dreaming, we have the sense of having a body, we observe other people and our environment, and we may experience all types of emotions. We can move from one place to another simply by a shift of consciousness. Such travel is not limited even by the speed of light. It is instantaneous. We think of a place and we are there, simultaneous with our thinking. Similarly, in the bardo state, one has a body that is made of the stuff that dreams are made of: it is purely a mental body, a creation of the mind. This mental body is replete with sense faculties, and with it one can observe other people and events in the bardo. As in the dream state, one can move as swiftly as thought, and one's vision is unimpeded, that is, where one looks, one sees.

Western scientists have investigated different types of dreaming. Most commonly the dreamer is unaware he is dreaming. In lucid dreaming, on the other hand, one is fully cognizant that one is dreaming. Tibetan Buddhists have long been aware of lucid dreaming and have worked to cultivate this ability. They have also explored techniques for detaching one's dream-body from one's physical body, and for employing this in various ways. This is an extremely useful preparation for entering the bardo state, and for deriving the greatest possible benefit from this experience.[10]

If one enters the intermediate state with a wholesome mind, it tends to be a very pleasant experience filled with light; whereas if one's mind is unwholesome, this transitional state is dark and foreboding. The type of body one takes in the bardo state corresponds to the type of rebirth that immediately follows. If one is about to take human rebirth, one's bardo body will be of a human form. The one exception occurs in the case of transmigrating to an immaterial realm. Such existence is not preceded by an intermediate state; one enters that dimension immediately following death.

Now let us look at the process of conception following the intermediate state, taking as an example rebirth as a human. According to Buddhism, as one comes to the end of the bardo period, one has a vision. This is not a perception of an event that is occurring in the human realm, but an illusory vision as in a dream. In it one sees the regenerative substances of one's parents-to-be, and one sees them in the act of sexual intercourse. This vision occurs whether or not they are engaging in this act, and the bardo being is lustfully drawn to this event. Moreover, Buddhism says, this lust is directed toward the parent of the opposite sex of that being which is about to be conceived. As one perceives only the copulating genitals, anger arises, and this brings an end to the intermediate state. One dies from the bardo state and is conceived as a human.

REBIRTH

To be reborn in a certain place one must be attracted to that place. So, for example, if one has no desire to be reborn in the United States, one will not be born there. The type of rebirth is a result of desire.

How does this accord with the Buddhist assertion that we are propelled into each rebirth by the power of karma, and not simply out of choice? Why, for instance, would anyone take birth as a nāraka? To answer this, let us consider the example of a person who loves to mutilate and kill. In the bardo state this person may witness a battlefield and be drawn to it by the force of habituation. This battlefield will actually be a vision of a naraka realm, and by desiring to enter into the conflict, this person will be reborn in that realm. In short, desire arises in close association with one's propulsive karma, which is determined by one's habitual behavior, and all these are instrumental in the process of taking rebirth.

While it may sound fantastic, this account of the six realms of sentient beings and the process of death, intermediate period, and rebirth is based upon the Buddha's teachings. It has been put to the test by many generations of Indian and Tibetan contemplatives, some of them *tulkus*, who have remembered the events leading to their birth. Many other contemplatives declare they have observed beings in all six realms by means of their heightened awareness. Is their experience authentic, or are they simply fantasizing? This judgment is best made by closely examining the type of meditative discipline that resulted in their experience. Is it a training that leads to greater mental clarity, stability, and discernment, or does it encourage self-deception and delusion? The Buddhist methods used by these contemplatives are available for our theoretical and empirical inspection.

The Buddha emphasized the unsatisfactory nature of rebirth in all these realms, and he encouraged followers to seek liberation from this cycle. This does not mean one longs for personal annihilation. This is not even possible, for the continuum of consciousness cannot be destroyed. It is possible, though, to have greater freedom in one's choice of rebirth, and eventually to become free of compulsive rebirth altogether.

Our present bodies are the fruition of our behavior in our past lives, and on the basis of the Buddha's teachings, we can study the relationships between specific types of deeds and their karmic results. For instance, the Buddha declared that a karmic result of patience is physical beauty and good health. Generosity gives rise to affluence in future lives. So, based upon our present circumstances, we can infer our behavioral patterns in previous lives. Similarly, we can infer the type of rebirth we will take based upon our present mental habits. If our minds are predominantly unwholesome, chances are we will take an unfortunate rebirth; and if our minds are usually wholesome, we will likely be reborn in one of the fortunate realms.

Who does and who does not achieve liberation in any one lifetime is not a matter of chance. One critical factor is the degree of spiritual maturity that one brings to this life from one's previous rebirths. This is generally very difficult to gauge, especially since the impressions from previous spiritual practices may remain latent throughout much of one's life, awaiting the proper catalyst for their emergence. A more evident influence on the rate of one's spiritual development is the quality and perseverance of one's practice in this life. All of us have the potential to achieve liberation, but few of us cultivate the outer and inner conditions necessary for this in this lifetime.

Motivation is crucial. We may engage in wholesome activity, but where will it lead us? To a pleasant celestial vacation in a deva realm? To rebirth as a belligerent asura, or to a human life in which we are surrounded by material prosperity but spiritual impoverishment? Where our wholesome karma leads us is largely determined by the motivation for our behavior. If we lead a wholesome life hoping we will acquire material gain, prestige, and influence in future lives, this is where our actions will lead. If our apparently virtuous deeds are aimed only at the eight worldly concerns in this life, they may satisfy that aspiration without yielding any benefits for future lives. This is true of meditation as well. If we practice in order to acquire clairvoyance or psychic powers, our meditations may be without significance in terms of actual spiritual development.

The karmic impressions from our past deeds can be likened to fuel that propels us from one life to another, but the motivation behind those deeds is like the steering mechanism. If our predominant incentive for spiritual practice is to attain the fullest possible spiritual awakening for the benefit of all beings, this is where the fruits of our labors will ripen. Even if many of our wholesome actions seem insignificant, their karmic power will further us along our spiritual paths not only in this life, but through all our lives, until Buddhahood is attained. Instead of leading to pointless pleasures in deva realms and so on, these wholesome karmic impressions will lead us to situations that are most conducive for our further spiritual unfolding. Striving to maintain this continuity of gradual awakening from one life to the next is far more important than counting on the attainment of Buddhahood in any one lifetime.

7

GATEWAY TO FREEDOM

LIBERATION FROM SUFFERING

In the preceding chapters we examined the first two of the Four Noble Truths—the truth of suffering and the truth of the source of suffering. The Buddha's teachings on these subjects make an overwhelming statement: the troubles we experience—the discontent, frustration, and misery—and the essential causes of suffering— ignorance, hatred, and attachment—can continue forever. The cycle of dissatisfaction is self-perpetuating. As long as we ignore the inner causes of suffering and devote our lives to mundane concerns, we will remain subject to misery.

If we take this assertion seriously, we are faced with this question: "Given that my stream of awareness is indestructible, is it possible to lessen, or even dispel completely my suffering and the mental distortions that cause suffering? Is it possible to become utterly free from the afflictions of the mind? In other words, is it possible to be thoroughly sane?"

The Buddha's response is: "Yes, this is possible."

We have the potential to be free of discontent because there is a way to identify its primary cause and to uproot it. This cause is ignorance, and the Buddha strongly emphasized the central role of ignorance that falsely conceives of an inherently existent self. The antidote for this ignorance is insight into the fact that the self that is conceived by ignorance does not really exist. Truly realizing the absence of an intrinsic self profoundly alters the mind. One who has gained such nonconceptual insight is called an *ārya,* and such a person is assured of eventual freedom from the cycle of existence.

Ignorance vanishes as one's mind is thoroughly saturated with that realization, through experiencing it repeatedly. As a result, the other mental afflictions that derive from ignorance also disappear. One is then freed not only from accumulating fresh karma, because attachment and repulsion are extinguished, but one is also freed from being propelled into future rebirths by the power of previous karma. In the absence of mental distortions, previous karma cannot be stimulated and come to fruition. A person who has gained this liberation is called an *arhat*.

There are two types of nirvāṇa, or liberation, called *nirvāṇa with remainder* and *nirvāṇa without remainder*. Nirvāṇa with remainder means that one still has a body. Let us imagine that you attain nirvāṇa at the age of fifty-two, and then you live another thirty years. For the rest of your life, there is no possibility you will be afflicted by any mental distortions. You will live with unblemished sanity.

Might you experience any pain? The Buddhist accounts of arhats suggest that they feel no mental distress, no fear or anxiety. The arhat does indeed feel physical sensations of pain, but he does not identify with them. Ignorance does not cling to those sensations with the idea that this is "my" body that is afflicted. So, while the pain is noted, it does not overwhelm the arhat's mind. There is awareness that the body is afflicted in the conventional sense, and the pain is serving a purpose by calling attention to the physical malady.

The common, definitive characteristic of all arhats is that they are free of mental distortions. But in terms of the virtuous qualities of wisdom and compassion, arhats' capacities differ widely from one to another. There were many arhats among the Buddha's disciples, and some were renowned for various outstanding virtues. Śāriputra, for example, was known as the wisest of all the arhat disciples, and Maudgalyāyana was exceptional for his supernormal powers and clairvoyance.

A final comment on nirvāṇa with remainder may be worth mentioning. Earlier the point was made that virtually all our experience of mundane pleasure is merely a decrease in discontent. Is it not also true, however, that all suffering is felt due to a lessening of joy? Are pleasure and pain relative? If so, how can arhats feel joy if they no longer have any unhappiness with which to compare it? In other words, if joy and sorrow are a duality like up and down, or high and low, would it not be impossible to identify one in the absence of the other?

To answer this, we should note that arhats do not lose their memory upon attaining liberation. They can remember their own suffering prior to their liberation, so their unprecedented state of well-being does occur in relation to their former discontent, and they can easily compare their state with that of others.

On a deeper level, it is important to recognize that the well-being emanating from an arhat's profound sanity is radically different from an ordinary person's happiness. The joys of those of us who are not liberated are normally contingent upon favorable external conditions; and we apprehend such pleasurable feelings as intrinsically "mine." The Buddha called such pleasure "tainted," and observed that it is actually a modification of suffering.

An arhat's joy, in contrast, arises from the profound sanity and equanimity of his own mind, free of the sense of an inherent "mine." It is a state of well-being that transcends the duality of tainted joy and sorrow and cannot be conceived or expressed by anyone whose experience is limited to that duality.

Although we cannot presently experience such transcendent joy, we can aspire to achieve it. Instead of going out to have fun, we can go in to find equanimity. Instead of trying to alter our environment and companions to alleviate our discontent, we can look inward to identify its cause. By calming the mind and by gaining a respite from the turbulence of compulsive thinking, we experience a fresh sense of well-being.

For unenlightened people this happiness is transient, because it depends upon the temporary stability and clarity of the mind. Sooner or later the mental distortions that underlie these qualities will disrupt our mental equanimity, and the resultant well-being will vanish. For this reason, the attainment of samādhi in Buddhist practice is seen, not as an end in itself, but as a useful state of awareness for exploring the essential nature of reality. The meditative insight thus attained opens up a more profound equanimity, an even deeper experience of well-being. This quality of existence becomes indestructible when the distortions of the mind are completely dispelled.

Until an arhat dies, he is said to have attained nirvāṇa with remainder, for he still has a body that was produced by karma. When he dies, he is freed of that body and all other fully matured effects of karma, and at this point there is nirvāṇa without remainder. What happens to this arhat? Is he annihilated, blown out like a candle? There are some who mistakenly assert this. They assume that since the arhat is liberated from all mental and physical effects of karma, including rebirth in the cycle of existence, such a person simply vanishes at death.

This interpretation of Buddhism deserves the label "world-negating." Those who adhere to it see all sentient existence as saturated by suffering, which motivates them to seek an end to existence. This suggests the entire universe is a cosmic tragedy, and the culmination of spiritual striving is to self-destruct with a thoroughness mere suicide is unable to achieve.

This nihilistic view of existence fails to penetrate the meaning of nirvāṇa as taught by the Buddha. The experience of nirvāṇa without remainder is beyond the scope of human concepts, including our reified ideas of existence and nonexistence. An arhat in this state is never again compelled to take rebirth because of karma, but, according to Tibetan Buddhism, the arhat may do so out of compassion. Such a being may also take rebirth in order to engage in practices that dispel the extremely subtle obscurations to omniscience. These are the final veils that must be removed to attain the complete spiritual awakening of a Buddha.

ENTERING THE PATH

Having expounded on the truth of suffering, its source, and its cessation, the Buddha taught the path to liberation and spiritual awakening. Before proceeding, it may be worth asking: Why should the cessation of suffering be the goal of our spiritual practice? Theistic religions emphasize union with God, while more philosophical traditions are concerned with gaining knowledge of Ultimate Truth. The yearning to be free of suffering may be seen as an expression of cowardice, with nothing particularly noble about it. Everyone wants to be free of pain, including toads and guppies. Should we not aspire for something more exalted?

At heart, the desire for union with God, for realization of Ultimate Truth, and for freedom from suffering through the complete purification of the mind, are different expressions of the same yearning. They may differ in profundity according to the depth of one's understanding, but they share much in common. Without arguing that the wish for freedom from suffering is necessarily a superior motivation, there are some practical advantages.

For one, the desire to be free of pain is indeed something we share in common with all sentient beings. Acknowledging this motivation for our spiritual quest reaffirms our kinship with living beings. We do not exalt ourselves as "spiritual people," raised above the masses. This sense of kinship is an aid to the practice of Dharma.

There is certainly nothing wrong with the noble aspiration for divine union or for an unmediated experience of Truth. However, there is a danger of seeing this as something separate and unrelated to the day-to-day events that fill our lives. What do such sublime quests have to do with our anxiety at finding that someone is bringing a lawsuit against us, or with conflicts with our spouse or children, or with myriad other problems and irritations?

It is essential to recognize that while the practice of Dharma leads to experiences that can be labeled as divine union or experience

79

of Ultimate Reality, it also offers practical means for responding with sanity to all the events of daily life. Learning to accept misfortune without dismay or hostility is a step toward ultimate transcendence.

When practiced from the ground up, Buddhadharma swiftly yields tangible benefits in our personal lives. We may not quickly penetrate to Ultimate Truth, but we do find that our behavior gradually reduces conflict in our own lives and with the people around us. Anger does not arise as frequently or as strongly, and with the lessening of attachment, our anxiety and stress also decrease. One result of these transformations is that we experience an increasing sense of equanimity and inner well-being.

The Buddha taught to help us bring about these changes in our lives. His role is not to judge us or punish us for our failings. Rather, he is known as the Great Physician. His task is to show sentient beings how to heal themselves from the mental afflictions and resultant unwholesome types of behavior that perpetuate pain and unhappiness.

TAKING REFUGE

The gateway to the Buddhist path of liberation is taking refuge in the Buddha, the Dharma, and the spiritual community, known as the *Saṅgha*. Taking refuge involves wholehearted commitment to this spiritual path and to the one who revealed it—the Buddha. This does not mean that one cannot engage in certain Buddhist practices without making such a commitment. A wide range of Buddhist methods can be practiced by people of other faiths and ideologies. But in terms of progressing along the Buddhist path, trust and commitment are essential.

The notion of taking refuge may appear strange until we recognize the many ways in which we have already taken refuge by placing our trust, faith, or confidence in other people, institutions, and so on. Most of us take refuge in banks by entrusting them with our savings.

For physical ailments we take refuge in doctors; we take refuge in the government to protect our homeland, to educate our children, and to give us a stipend in our old age.

Before considering the Buddhist practice of taking refuge, let us pause and reflect: To what do we already entrust ourselves, and what fruits have we reaped from this trust?

In Buddhism we speak of temporal and ultimate refuge. Recognizing a mundane, or temporal problem, we may take refuge in someone or something that is able to protect us from harm or extricate us from a present difficulty. Devout Buddhists, for example, will not hesitate to take temporal refuge in a doctor when they are ill. Temporal refuge, therefore, pertains to a broad range of issues about our well-being in this life alone.

Ultimate refuge, on the other hand, focuses on our welfare beyond this life. We take ultimate refuge to protect us from dangers in future lives, to sever the roots of discontent, and to unveil our full potential for spiritual awakening.

In the context of Buddhism, there are two causes for taking refuge: the first is a clear recognition of our present situation; the second is seeing that help is available.

In the first case, we can start by looking into our own minds, which we know are frequently afflicted by mental distortions. Examining our behavior, we note that it, too, is often unwholesome. We may accept the Buddha's observation that the future karmic impressions from these actions will be disastrous. Thus, to recognize our present situation is to see we are in peril, in terms of this and future lifetimes.

Recognizing this personal predicament does not necessarily cause us to take refuge in the Buddha or any other spiritual leader. Some spiritually inclined people feel the teachings of the world's religions are antiquated and therefore no longer relevant to the modern world. Others refuse to commit themselves, doubting the authenticity of spiritual teachings so far removed in time from the original teachers. Their solution is often to take ultimate refuge in themselves, while experimenting with a variety of practices from one or more spiritual traditions.

The fact that the fundamental distortion of the mind creates a false sense of personal identity further complicates the problem. The rugged individualist may set out on the spiritual path with the resolve: "I want to heal my mind of my false sense of I." Imagine that this person practices meditation and gains a heightened degree of mental stability and clarity, and acquires a great deal of spiritual learning. There is a great danger that each of these attainments will serve only to inflate this person's false sense of selfhood. So, while striving diligently on the spiritual path, he is in fact nurturing the very root of his mental distortions and suffering.

The first cause of taking refuge is to recognize our present peril and our inability to free ourselves on our own. The second cause is to acknowledge that help is available and to entrust ourselves to those sources of refuge.

The chief objects of refuge in Buddhist practice are the Buddha, the Dharma, or spiritual path that he revealed, and the Saṅgha, or spiritual community of āryas. Taking refuge in these "Three Jewels" is to place our trust in them, confident they will not mislead us. This step does not entail a blind leap of faith, nor does it require a complete understanding of the qualities of the Three Jewels.

Generally speaking, there are two ways to develop faith in the Three Jewels. One is through learning about the qualities of the Buddha and the life he led, the other is through testing the Buddha's teachings in one's own experience and understanding.

In the Buddhist scriptures we can read of the compassion and wisdom the Buddha expressed toward others, even those who were intent on his downfall, and there are many accounts of his extraordinary powers and heightened awareness.

Developing faith in this way is very personal, similar to the faith that one may develop when observing the noble qualities of one's own spiritual mentor. We may feel these teachings are authentic due to the extraordinary qualities of the person who is their source, and we may entrust ourselves to the Dharma due to our faith in a mentor, who represents a Buddha.

The other approach to faith is through investigating the Buddhist world view, critically examining its tenets by means of logic and reasoning. We must test the practices taught by the Buddha, and witness for ourselves the transformations they bring about. In this way we may experience a growing appreciation and reverence for the Buddhadharma, and this leads to faith in its source, the Buddha.

The Objects of Refuge

What is it that makes the Buddha, Dharma, and Sangha worthy objects of refuge? A Buddha, first of all, is free not only of all mental distortions, as are arhats, but of even subtler cognitive obscurations. Buddhas are forever free of all fear and danger and are skillful in leading others to freedom. They feel great compassion toward all living creatures, and offer Dharma to everyone without discrimination. Regardless of what we have or have not done to the Buddhas, they show no favoritism but treat all with equal loving concern.

The historical Buddha is the source of the Dharma to which Buddhists entrust themselves. The Dharma can be understood in two ways: as spiritual realization and as the teachings that lead to such realization.

The Sangha originates from the practice of Dharma. Strictly speaking, the Sangha refers only to āryas who have gained a non-conceptual realization of ultimate truth. More loosely, it refers to the community of spiritual practitioners. Fellow practitioners can be a vital aid to us as we progress along the path, for many of them are far more advanced than we, and even those at our own level may have special insights to share with us. They offer us experiential guidance and act as living examples of the practice of Dharma. Finally, they can be a great source of inspiration, for in them we can see the tangible benefits of spiritual practice.

The refuges of the Buddha, Dharma, and Saṅgha can be understood using a common analogy in Tibetan Buddhism. We go for refuge out of need, like a person afflicted with countless diseases. The Buddha can then be likened to a physician, the Dharma to the medical treatment and therapy, and the Saṅgha to the nurses who care for us. The Buddha's chief task is to reveal the Dharma, and the Saṅgha's is to assist us in our practice. The most direct refuge is the Dharma.

How do we go about taking refuge in the Three Jewels? If we recognize our personal need for refuge and entrust ourselves to the Buddha, Dharma, and Saṅgha, we have taken refuge. We are now Buddhist. We may celebrate this step by participating in a ritual of taking refuge with a spiritual mentor, but the ritual is not essential. And if we have not inwardly taken refuge, the external ritual is meaningless.

THE SPIRITUAL MENTOR

Now let us imagine that someone has taken heartfelt refuge in the Three Jewels and is ready to set forth on the Buddhist path of liberation. Is it necessary to seek out a spiritual mentor for personal guidance on the path? Nowadays in the West, the term *Guru* has become burdened with accounts of personality cults, exploitation, manipulation, and fraud. Therefore, we should begin by acknowledging that Buddhists are not required to have a Guru.

In the Buddhist context the term *Guru* means spiritual mentor, and the Tibetan translation of this term is *Lama*. The Sanskrit word literally means "heavy," suggesting a fullness of virtue and insight, while the Tibetan term suggests one who is unsurpassed in virtue.

Of what use is a spiritual mentor? Let us say we wish to learn a skill such as making cabinets. There is no law that says we have to study under a master cabinetmaker; we can buy books on the subject, purchase our own tools, and teach ourselves. But in depriving ourselves of another's personal assistance, we may waste a lot of time. A master artisan can quickly help us to identify and correct the flaws in our work; something a book cannot do. This means that with the same amount of effort, we can more swiftly master the essentials and develop our own creative skills.

The more subtle and sophisticated the skill or discipline, the greater the need for a teacher. The discipline of Buddhadharma includes psychological research, philosophical inquiry, moral decisions, and extensive, demanding training in meditation. There is perhaps no body of knowledge and practice that is more subtle or sophisticated. This spiritual path is designed to free our minds completely of all distortions; and yet we must use our afflicted minds to bring this about. Here is a tremendous challenge, and to succeed we need all the help we can get.

Let us imagine that we are resolved to achieve liberation by means of the Buddhadharma, and we want to find a suitable mentor. Ideally we should find a Buddha, for such a being is best equipped to speed us along our path. Indeed, while Buddha Śākyamuni was living, his guidance was so skillful that he led thousands of people to freedom. So if we can find a Buddha to be our teacher, we need look no further.

If we cannot find a Buddha who is free of all obscurations and replete with all virtues, we may seek out an arhat who is liberated from all mental distortions. Such a teacher will not be as skillful as a Buddha, but that person will still have personal experience of the entire path to nirvāṇa; so his or her credentials as a spiritual mentor will still be formidable.

It can be difficult to find Buddhas and arhats nowadays. Not all truly liberated beings proclaim their own state of realization, and many people who do claim to be enlightened are in fact deluded. If we cannot find a Buddha or an arhat, what essential qualities shall we look for in a spiritual mentor? This person should be well versed in the theory and practice of the three trainings that form the core of the Buddhadharma and should practice them in his or her own life.

The first of these three trainings is moral discipline. A qualified spiritual mentor is one who leads a wholesome way of life, avoids harming others and serves them whenever possible. He should also be knowledgeable about the relationships between actions and their karmic results—the moral laws of nature that the Buddha observed and taught. Second, a Guru should be well trained in the methods for cultivating meditative stability and clarity. Finally, he should be thoroughly acquainted with the Buddha's teachings on identitylessness, and should be experienced in the cultivation of meditative insight.

If we find someone teaching Dharma, it is well worth asking, "Why is he doing it? What is his motivation?" If he is teaching for personal gain, for prestige, or for power over others, he is not a teacher of the Buddhadharma but rather of the eight worldly concerns. An authentic spiritual mentor guides others from a motivation of compassion.

If a person is well versed in the three trainings of moral discipline, meditative stabilization, and wisdom, and teaches out of kindness, he is an authentic spiritual mentor. It is not always easy to recognize these characteristics. Sometimes they may be present in a Guru, but we fail to recognize them; and other times they may be lacking, but we imagine that they are there.

Such are the essential attributes of an authentic spiritual mentor. What are the necessary characteristics of a qualified student of Dharma? In order for the relationship between the two to be fruitful, the pupil must also be well prepared. Otherwise the association may prove to be unfruitful.

Buddhist treatises speak of just three prerequisites on the part of the student. The first of these is a lack of bias or prejudice. This implies, among other things, that the student does not cling to his own assumptions and beliefs simply because they are his. He seeks guidance from his mentor in a spirit of humility and open-mindedness.

The second quality is intelligence, or discernment. Buddhist training calls for keen perceptiveness as we explore the teachings and enter into the practice. It is not enough simply to have faith and blindly follow orders.

The third quality is aspiration. It is not enough for a student to study Dharma simply as an intellectual pursuit. One's motivation needs to be more than curiosity or the desire to acquire knowledge; one must aspire to put the teachings into practice and to experience the fruits of the path.

If a student has these three qualities, he will be well equipped to recognize the wholesome qualities of his mentor. Otherwise, the teacher's failings may be seen as virtues, and his virtues seen as shortcomings.

The extent to which we are able to benefit from having a Guru hinges not only on his accomplishments but also on the depth of our own faith and trust. A teacher's knowledge may be very limited, but if we sincerely entrust ourselves to his guidance, we may find that wonderful transformations take place in our lives. On the other hand, someone else may have profound insight and compassion and be an extremely skillful teacher; yet if we lack faith, we may receive virtually no benefit at all.

The responsibility of a Guru is to care for the spiritual welfare of his students to the best of his ability. The responsibility of the student is to serve his teacher. This service includes seeing that the physical needs of his teacher are met. But the most important way of serving one's mentor is to put his teachings into practice as well as one can.

Nowadays the issue of serving one's Guru is a delicate one, for we have heard many accounts of so-called Gurus exploiting their devotees by demanding their money, obedience, and adulation. An authentic spiritual mentor's primary source of satisfaction from guiding students is seeing them benefit from the Dharma. He is most pleased by their wholehearted dedication to spiritual practice, not by their material offerings. And yet, service to one's mentor also has an important place in Dharma. For if students give nothing of value in return for spiritual guidance, the benefit they receive from their mentor may be very limited. Here it is not a case of the Guru exploiting his students, but of the students exploiting their Guru.

How shall we regard our spiritual mentor? Buddhist tradition offers a variety of answers to this question, but a suitable attitude in the beginning stages of practice is this: regard the teacher as a representative of the Buddha. We cannot have the historical Buddha as our personal mentor, so the closest approximation is a qualified teacher to whom we should devote ourselves, since he has been trained in an unbroken lineage of the Buddhadharma. Such a person has become a vessel of the Buddha's words and represents for us his wisdom and compassion.

It is the teacher's responsibility to transmit the Buddhadharma without distortion, and to adapt its form to make it meaningful to the lives of his students. If this is done, it is quite possible some of his students may gain deeper realization than himself, for the Dharma he has transmitted may contain knowledge beyond his own limited experience.

What does it mean to regard one's mentor as a representative of the Buddha? Imagine receiving a personal emissary from the highly esteemed president of a powerful nation. This emissary may not have the outstanding personal qualities of the president, and he may have numerous shortcomings as an individual. And yet we do not look upon him simply as an isolated person. He is the mouthpiece of the president, and in this sense the emissary wields his authority. Therefore, we honor him for his role as a representative, paying little regard to his personal failings. And for his part the emissary accepts this honor, recognizing it is not directed to him personally. Similarly, it is suitable to honor one's spiritual mentor as a representative, or emissary, of the Buddha.

We have spoken at length about taking external refuge in the Buddha, Dharma, and Saṅgha and in devoting ourselves to a spiritual mentor. But such outer refuges must be complemented by the inner cultivation of our own wisdom. When we are separated from our teachers, we must rely upon our own insight and judgment—this, too, must be our refuge.

How shall we apply the teachings to the specific, unique events that make up our daily lives? No external Guru can guide us in our responses to these situations from moment to moment. We must take refuge in our own wisdom, which becomes our inner Guru. In a fruitful relationship between a mentor and a student, the latter grows in self-reliance. The culmination of this development occurs when the student's wisdom merges inseparably with that of his mentor. This union takes place when the student becomes a Buddha. At this point one has become a source of refuge for others, and the stream of service continues.

8

THE FOUNDATION OF SPIRITUAL PRACTICE

Taking refuge in the Buddha, Dharma, and Saṅgha is the gateway to the Buddhist spiritual path. The specific aspects of spiritual practice, or the path, have a common, indispensable foundation. That foundation is the cultivation of a wholesome, or ethical, way of life. In Buddhism this is often referred to as moral discipline.

If we were to spend an entire lifetime focusing only on establishing this foundation in our daily lives, we would have begun a sound spiritual practice that would yield great benefits in this and future lives. However, if we were to try many of the other practices described in the following chapters, while overlooking this foundation, our efforts would be like building on quicksand.

The initial emphasis of moral discipline is on restraint from unwholesome behavior; namely, that which harms ourselves and others. The second emphasis is on service to others.

This emphasis on moral restraint raises a serious doubt in many people's minds today: "If we are supposed to base our lives on a set of prohibitory rules, our natural spontaneity will be curtailed. How can a spiritual path that restrains our personal freedom lead to liberation?" To respond to this, let us take a look at some of the expressions of our "natural" spontaneity. Imagine we have just bought a new car, and a few days later we see someone ram into our opened car door because it is blocking that person's way out of a parking lot. For many of us our spontaneous reaction would be rage, and this might compel us to retaliate. While in the throes of this mental affliction we are anything but free, yet we are acting "spontaneously." The point is obvious: much of our "personal spontaneity" is dominated by mental distortions, which lead to unwholesome behavior that harms ourselves and others. We are bound by these afflictions. Buddhist practice, beginning with moral restraint, is designed to liberate us from these sources of misery. From the Buddhist perspective this kind of "spontaneity" is nothing of the kind; in fact it is a form of suffering, the first of the Four Noble Truths and the starting place of the Buddha's teachings.

It is true that some of our spontaneity is wholesome, and our challenge is to shift all our natural responses toward this wholesomeness. Sometimes our painful mental habits are so rigid that they feel like they are carved in stone. And yet the flow of our thoughts and emotions is constantly changing from moment to moment, flowing like a mountain brook. How can we direct the stream of our behavior out of its habitual grooves into the ways of thoroughly wholesome spontaneity? By persistent, continuous effort.

This is very hard at the beginning, and sometimes discouraging. But gradually we can change how we think. Our old unwholesome habits will not assert themselves quite so automatically; and our thoughts, emotions, and other behavior will tend toward greater sanity. The key to this powerful transition is consistent spiritual practice, which leads to harmonious spontaneity and true freedom.

MORAL DISCIPLINE AND SPIRITUAL GROWTH

The Buddhist path of spiritual awakening includes many practices designed to bring about deep transformations in consciousness, ranging from methods for stabilizing the mind to ways of cultivating insight and compassion. Many spiritual aspirants have discovered for themselves that if they fail to establish a basis of moral discipline, these practices are simply not effective. Without this moral foundation, powerful unwholesome tendencies that remain in the mind may be easily triggered by employing powerful meditative techniques. When this happens, one may suddenly fall ill, or suffer great psychological trauma. Sometimes these afflictions vanish as soon as one withdraws from the practice that triggered them; but they may so disrupt one's nervous system that harmful symptoms may remain for years.

There are less drastic signs that one's degree of moral discipline does not provide sufficient support for one's spiritual growth. For instance, as a result of one's meditation and devotions one may experience moments of a radical shift of consciousness. One's sense of duality between subject and object may suddenly vanish; one may experience a spontaneous out-flowing of love for all beings; or one may feel an awesome current of power flowing from a seemingly fathomless source. However, if the ethical quality of one's life does not provide a harmonious context for these sublime experiences they will swiftly vanish, like a seed that germinates in poor soil.

An authentic motivation for spiritual practice does not focus chiefly on the visible benefits one attains in this life. Instead, it is more concerned with the long-term effects in future existences, reaching over one's entire path of awakening during many lifetimes. It is in this light that the importance of moral discipline is most crucial. Without this foundation—regardless of the alleged profundity of one's spiritual practice or esoteric techniques—there is little chance of having future rebirths that are favorable for spiritual practice.

According to Buddhist teachings, if one is reborn into an unfavorable realm of existence due to a lack of moral discipline, one's practice of Dharma is bound to grind to a halt. Once this happens, it may be many lifetimes before favorable conditions arise again so that practice can continue.

Establishing a foundation of moral discipline through the cultivation of virtuous behavior brings inner harmony in one's thoughts, emotions, and behavior. One experiences a refreshing serenity that is calm and filled with vitality, a quality that transforms one's relationships with others. Interpersonal strife and conflict are subdued, and a spirit of friendly cooperation arises spontaneously.

As mentioned previously, Buddhist ethics first emphasize restraint more than "doing good." At the beginning we must recognize how our mental, verbal, and physical behaviors create disharmony in our own lives and in our interactions with others. We can spend a great deal of energy on ingenious exercises, therapies, and other techniques for coping with stress and anxiety. But as long as we persist in the unwholesome behavior that actually produces these problems, no true healing will take place.

The seeds of virtue are already present in our minds. Moral restraint prepares the ground, removing the rocks and weeds of unwholesome behavior that impede the germination of these seeds. It creates space for them to grow. Spiritual growth is no act of will, nor a direct product of therapy or spiritual techniques. Instead, it is a blossoming of perfection already within us that we set free by spiritual practice, the foundation of which is morality.

TEN UNWHOLESOME DEEDS

A sound ethical basis for spiritual practice can be lived by avoiding what Buddhists call the *ten unwholesome deeds*. These ten were emphasized by the Buddha, for he realized they have especially harmful effects in this and in future lives. In setting forth moral guidelines, the Buddha's role is not that of a lawmaker or a judge, but of a physician. Just as a doctor counsels a patient to avoid certain types of behavior that aggravate his condition, so the Buddha advised his followers in moral restraint.

Classical Tibetan medical treatises, which Tibetans believe to be rooted in the Buddha's teachings, are based on morality. They start by prescribing certain behaviors, diets, and so on for people with specific maladies. Then, prescribing according to various metabolisms, they give more general instructions for preventing illness before it occurs. Finally, they offer fundamental advice on behavior that will lead to good health in this and future lives. This behavior consists of restraint from the ten unwholesome deeds, as taught by the Buddha.

According to Tibetan medicine, all physical disorders fundamentally stem from ignorance, attachment, and hatred. So if one seeks a lasting state of good health, one must overcome these underlying afflictions.

During the early 1970s, I had the privilege of spending a year in the home of Yeshe Dönden, a Tibetan doctor who was at that time the personal physician of His Holiness the Dalai Lama. Once I asked him, "What's the relationship between Tibetan medicine and Dharma?" He looked at me with amused surprise and replied emphatically, "This medicine *is* Dharma!"

Let us take a look at the restraint from the ten unwholesome deeds that forms the basis of Buddhist ethics. The first three deeds are physical actions, the next four verbal, and the final three are mental.

The first of the ten unwholesome actions is taking the life of a sentient being. This does not include plants. While Buddhism recognizes plants as living, it does not regard them as sentient, conscious beings. So, harvesting a crop of wheat, for example, is not regarded as killing.

To accumulate the karma of killing, so that the impressions placed on one's mindstream from this deed are fully potent, four factors must be present when the act is committed.

The first of these is called the *necessary condition*; in this case, another sentient being to kill.

Second is the *intent*, which includes recognition by the killer that the object to be killed is a sentient being. The intent also must be dominated by a mental distortion, be it ignorance, attachment, or anger; and there must be the intent to kill.

Third is the *enactment* of the deed, that is, the procedure one follows. The procedure may be direct, as when one slaps a mosquito or shoots a deer; or it may be indirect, by ordering someone else to kill. For example, the commanding officer of soldiers in battle is karmically responsible, together with his troops, for all the killing that he supervises, even though he never fires a shot himself.

The fourth factor is the *completion* of the act: one's victim dies before oneself.

The second of these ten unwholesome deeds is stealing, or more literally, taking that which is not given. The necessary condition is something that belongs to someone else. One recognizes this, and one takes steps to acquire it. Simply robbing the other person's possession is a very blatant method, but far more devious means of trickery and cheating also may be used. The completion of the act occurs when one thinks, "Now it's mine."

When these four factors of stealing are present, karmic impressions are placed upon the mindstream which will certainly bring personal misfortune in this or future lives, unless steps are taken to neutralize their potency.

The third deed is sexual misconduct. This includes a variety of sexually related behavior, but this is not the time for a very detailed explanation. The principal form of sexual misconduct is entering into sexual relations with someone else's spouse. Another is sexual intercourse with a child or youth who is still under his or her parents' care. The necessary condition, intent, enactment, and completion can all be surmised on the basis of the previous examples of killing and stealing.

Of the four verbal unwholesome deeds, the first is lying. This may be vocal, but it also includes intentionally misleading someone with a nod or a gesture. One may even lie by keeping silent.

Slander, the second of the verbal deeds, depends on motivation. Imagine two individuals, or it could be two or more communities, who have a harmonious relationship. If one speaks with the intention of creating disharmony or distrust between them, this is slander. Or if two parties are already at odds, and one speaks in order to prevent a reconciliation between them, this too is slander. Such speech may be true or false—it is still slander.

The third of these verbal acts is abuse. As with slander, what determines whether one's words are abusive is one's motivation. If one speaks with the intention to inflict harm, this is abuse; and, as we know, this may bring greater suffering to another person than physical injury. The abuse may be directed toward the person with whom one is speaking, or it may be directed to someone else. In either case, as soon as one utters words in order to inflict harm, one accumulates the karma of abuse.

With this brief introduction to slander and abuse, let us review our own verbal behavior. We may find that on occasion we do speak of the faults of others, saying so-and-so is conceited, aggressive, or selfish. As soon as we speak about the faults of another person with an unwholesome motivation, it is guaranteed our speech is unwholesome. It is bound to be abusive or slanderous, and if we exaggerate, we also accumulate the karma of lying.

So we may ask: "When is it appropriate to speak about the faults of other people?" The answer is: "Hardly ever." If at times we feel it necessary to speak of someone's faults, we are well advised to look first into our own hearts to see if we are motivated by any mental distortion. If we find our intention is thoroughly wholesome, that we sincerely wish to speak out of a desire to benefit the other person, then we may proceed, drawing on our full capacity of wisdom and kindness.

Many people find that by this simple act of discipline, their minds become more serene. Try to recall a person who rarely or never speaks of others' faults. We can feel very much at ease with this person, because if we never hear him or her speak of others' shortcomings, we can feel confident the person is not abusing us behind our backs either. Such simple restraint creates harmony in the mind of the person who practices it, and it is refreshing for others as well.

Idle gossip is the fourth of the verbal misdeeds. For speech to be included under this heading, it must be stimulated by a mental distortion. So, if we engage in friendly, casual conversation, we need not fear we are doing something unwholesome. But if our speech is dominated by any mental distortion, including attachment, it is bound to be a form of idle gossip, even if it is not included in the other three verbal misdeeds. Moreover, unlike the other three, one can accumulate the karma of idle gossip without anyone else hearing one's words. Tibetan Buddhist teachers often comment that idle gossip is the most innocuous of the ten unwholesome deeds, but it also provides the easiest way to waste one's life.

The first of the three mental unwholesome actions is avarice. This entails focusing on someone else's possession, and wishing it could be one's own. This act is entirely mental, and it is completed when one thinks, "Might that object be mine."

Malice is the second of the three mental nonvirtues. One engages in this unwholesome act whenever one wishes ill on another living being. Malice may be very focused in the sense of intending to bring misfortune to another person, or it may be a more general attitude of hoping someone will fall on bad times.

What can we do when such thoughts invade our minds? We may wish to lead wholesome, ethical lives, and yet at times our minds go out of control, carried away by mental distortions. We already have latent tendencies for avarice and malice, and when these are stimulated by outer events or by memory, emotions such as anger, resentment, and craving arise. We do not choose for them to occur, they simply arise in dependence on inner and outer conditions. However, once they have arisen, we do have a choice as to whether or not we identify with these unwholesome thoughts and emotions and apply energy to them.

With practice, it is possible to observe the arising of unwholesome thoughts and refuse to go along with them. It should be clearly understood that repression occurs when we refuse to acknowledge unwholesome mental tendencies. This plays no role in Buddhist practice. Rather, we are encouraged to acknowledge clearly the presence of any mental distortions that arise, to recognize that they are not inherently "I" or "mine," and finally to avoid giving effort to the perpetuation or increase of those distortions. The Indian sage Śāntideva writes on this theme:

> Whenever I wish to move
> Or to speak,
> First I shall examine my mind,
> And firmly act in a suitable way.
>
> Whenever my mind becomes attached
> Or angry,
> I shall not act, nor shall I speak.
> I shall remain like a piece of wood.[11]

The last of the ten unwholesome deeds is called false views. Holding onto a false view means denying the existence of something that does exist. For example, denying the continuity of awareness beyond death, denying that actions have any significance beyond their results in this life alone, and denying the possibility of freedom from mental distortions and their consequences—to Buddhists all of these are false views, and adhering to them brings misfortune.

COUNTERING THE UNWHOLESOME

If we wish to establish an ethical foundation for our Buddhist practice, it is essential to avoid these ten unwholesome deeds. We can learn about them and memorize the major points in the abstract, but the real challenge is to apply this understanding in daily life.

Some of those deeds, like killing and sexual misconduct, are easily identified, and refraining from them demands vigilance and control. But others, especially avarice and malice, may be very subtle, and even identifying them may be difficult.

Let us consider malice, for instance. If we think about it, we are bound to note occasions when we hope another person will be "put in his place" or lose face. Now, instead of simply going with this emotion, it is vital to stand back from it and openly acknowledge: "This is malice. This is not something confined to a book on Buddhism; it is not an abstract mental distortion; it is something that is dominating the way I think about this person." It is helpful to note how this mental activity affects our minds. Is it peaceful? Are we content? Is our intelligence operating clearly?

We may similarly observe how avarice influences our state of being. When the Buddha spoke of these as unwholesome, he was not referring only to their harmful effects in future lives. They also injure us in this life. The damage begins as soon as the mental distortions underlying them become active.

As we put these teachings into practice they come alive, and we discover for ourselves the pragmatic benefit of refraining from unwholesome behavior. We learn how difficult it can be even to recognize unwholesome behavior, and we find, too, that some unwholesome tendencies run very deep. Seeing the extent of the problem arouses greater interest in learning more about methods for overcoming these tendencies.

PURIFYING UNWHOLESOME KARMIC IMPRINTS

As soon as one engages in an unwholesome deed, impressions are placed on one's mindstream that will certainly result in misfortune, unless the power of those impressions is neutralized. Although a past unwholesome deed cannot be undone, the karmic impressions that are created can be presently subdued and even made completely impotent. In Buddhist practice this is done by the four remedial powers. This practice can overcome even the most powerful negative impressions.

The first of the four remedial powers is remorse. It is vital to make a clear distinction between this and guilt, another common response to misdeeds. Remorse focuses on a deed, recognizing it to be unwholesome and harmful in this and future lifetimes. The spirit of remorse can be understood using an analogy from the Tibetan tradition of Buddhism. Imagine three people coming into a restaurant and ordering the same meal. One of them begins eating first, several minutes later the second begins his meal, and finally the third begins his. After the third person has eaten just a few bites, the first person clutches at his abdomen, crying out in pain; and the second begins to show signs of discomfort.

How does the third person react? Not with guilt, or self-condemnation. Instead, he naturally regrets that he has eaten the same food as his two companions, but rather than dwelling on the past he moves rapidly to counter the effects of the poisonous food he has just eaten. His remorse is constructive. It is based in the present; it is intelligently concerned with the future effects of his recent actions; and it leads to remedying the damage already done and to caution about repeating such an act.

Guilt, in contrast, is usually a negative focus upon oneself: "I am an evil person. I can't bear myself. I am unworthy." While this response may appear in a religious guise, it often turns out to be a form of self-deprecating laziness. In Buddhism this is regarded as just one more mental distortion.

Proper remorse begins the process of purification by countering any tendency toward taking satisfaction in one's unwholesome action. This is crucial, for if one rejoices in any action, good or bad, it further empowers the karmic impressions from that action.

The second of the four remedial powers is applying an antidote to the unwholesome deed. In the broadest sense, this includes all wholesome activity, for all virtue counteracts the harmful impressions stored in the mindstream. The more wholesome the deed, the more powerfully it overcomes the mental afflictions. The cultivation of insight into the nature of reality and the cultivation of loving kindness are both very powerful antidotes.

The third remedial power is the resolve to avoid such harmful activity in the future. If the unwholesome deed in question is of a gross nature, such as killing or stealing, it is possible to resolve to stop these acts altogether. If the action is more subtle, or if one is very strongly habituated to it, it may be impossible to promise oneself that one will never do it again. In this case it is best to resolve to withdraw gradually from such behavior.

The fourth of these remedies is called the power of reliance. At times one may act in an unwholesome way toward a holy being, toward the Dharma, or toward one's spiritual friends. Here the power of reliance for a Buddhist means taking refuge in, or relying on, the Buddha, Dharma, and Saṅgha. On other occasions one may behave harmfully toward another sentient being, human or otherwise (apart from the Saṅgha); and the remedy for this is to place one's reliance in the cultivation of kindness and compassion toward others.

By applying these four remedial powers, any harmful karmic impression can be neutralized. If an unwholesome deed is especially powerful, this purification process may cause its karmic seeds to ripen in the form of a bad dream or an illness, instead of the miserable rebirth that it would otherwise have caused. Or, if one takes only halfhearted steps toward neutralizing the misdeed that one has committed, its karmic effects may be diminished, but not eliminated.

We can look for signs that we are actually purifying unwholesome impressions on our mindstreams. One of these is obvious: the decrease or elimination of unwholesome behavior such as the ten unwholesome deeds. Signs of purification also manifest in dreams, such as dreams of vomiting bad food, drinking milk or eating yogurt, seeing the sun or moon, dreaming that one is flying or that one's body is on fire. If any of these dreams occur repeatedly in the course of spiritual practice, this suggests that one's mindstream is being purified of unwholesome imprints.

ESTABLISHING THE BASIS OF SPIRITUAL GROWTH

The Buddha emphasized four themes of practice that can be very helpful and inspiring in cultivating a wholesome way of life.

The first of these is called *confidence of the heart,* which arises from moral purity. Moral purity here does not mean that one never commits an unwholesome deed; instead it means that one earnestly seeks to avoid the unwholesome and to purify it when it occurs.

The second theme is *guarding the doors of the senses.* Especially in early stages of Dharma practice, it is better to avoid situations that strongly stimulate mental distortions. This by itself is no cure for mental afflictions, but it does give us the space to cultivate wholesome antidotes to those afflictions. This is the rationale for monks removing themselves to monasteries and contemplatives living in solitude.

Sometimes, however, we meet unwholesome conditions unintentionally, and at those times it is especially vital to guard the senses. Then we should avoid looking at, or listening to, things that stimulate attachment and anger. Guarding the senses also means guarding the mind. For example, we may begin reflecting on the injury someone has done to us, and before long we are working ourselves into a rage. Such thinking is simply a way of harming ourselves.

Restraining the mind in such a situation means turning one's attention away from the object that is triggering one's afflictions. This requires *mindfulness* in the sense of being aware of what our mind is doing; and it requires *vigilance* in the sense of being on guard against indulging in unwholesome mental activity. These two qualities of awareness constitute the third of the four themes.

Without mindfulness and vigilance we do not have any spiritual practice at all. We may read and understand this account of Buddhist ethics, but as soon as we put this book down, our knowledge becomes history. We may engage in abuse, slander, deception, and so on, but without mindfulness we will be unaware they are taking place, and without vigilance the doors of our well-being will be battered down by these misdeeds. It is these two mental factors that create the link between the teachings and our lives.

Mindfulness offers us the choice to refrain from behavior that is damaging to ourselves and others. Without it, we are bound to react mechanically to favorable conditions with attachment, and to the unfavorable with hostility. Mindfulness is the door to freedom, and vigilance is the first step through that door—paradoxically, a step of restraint.

The fourth theme is leading a life of *simplicity* and *contentment,* and the benefits of such a life should be—at least for those interested in Buddhism—self-explanatory.

9

STABILIZING THE MIND

THE PURPOSE OF MEDITATIVE QUIESCENCE

Suppose that each of us wore a device that picked up all our thoughts, even the most subtle, unintentional ones, and immediately blared them out through loudspeakers strapped to the tops of our heads. As long as these thoughts remain hidden, often even from ourselves, we are able to present a fine semblance of sanity to those around us. But for most of us this veneer would swiftly vanish if others could hear the chaotic turbulence of our minds.

The whole of spiritual practice can be seen as cultivation of deeper and deeper sanity. In Buddhism this path of making the mind sane is a gradual one, beginning with relatively easy practices that bring about obvious, tangible benefits. The first stage of practice is ethical discipline, discussed in the previous chapter. The direct, manifest result of a life focused on these ethical principles is a greater state of well-being for ourselves and for those around us. Even without deep study or meditation, this brings about greater sanity and contentment.

As a result of this foundation of spiritual practice, our thoughts will be more wholesome, but our minds may still be scattered, unstable, and unclear. It is helpful to reinforce this foundation further by stabilizing our minds in meditation. In Buddhism the result of this practice is called *meditative quiescence,* or *tranquillity.* One contemplative of the Kagyüpa order of Tibetan Buddhism sums up tranquillity practice as follows:

> Tranquillity is achieved by focusing the mind on an
> object and maintaining it in that state until finally it is
> channeled into one stream of attention and evenness.[12]

Thus, in the Buddhist context, meditative quiescence means more than just a peaceful feeling. It is a quality of awareness that is stable and vivid, clearly focused upon its chosen object. It is not an end in itself, but a fine tool to be employed in the third phase of traditional Buddhist practice, namely, insight. The same author says of insight practice:

> Insight is attained through a general and detailed exami-
> nation of reality and the systematic application of intel-
> lectual discrimination.[13]

Experiential insight into the nature of reality is the direct anti-dote to ignorance, the mental affliction that lies at the root of all distortions of the mind, unwholesome behavior, and suffering. However, without achieving meditative quiescence, the healing power of insight is limited, and ignorance cannot be fully dispelled.

The Kagyüpa order, known for its emphasis on meditation, passes on such adages as "Where there is no contemplative tranquil-lity, there is no insight," and "If one seeks insight too early, one will not achieve tranquillity."[14] This Tibetan approach is very much in accord with the earlier Buddhism of India, as evidenced by the comments of the great Indian pandit Asaṅga regarding meditative quiescence and insight:

> What is tranquillity? It is to settle the mind in tranquil-
> lity, regularly, attentively, intensely; to clear the mind;
> to pacify the mind completely; and to settle the mind
> in one-pointedness and equipoise...
> What is insight? Insight is that which differentiates
> systematically and fully all things.... [15]

Certainly it is possible to gain some degree of insight without having achieved great mental stability, but such illumination is like the light of a candle flickering in a breeze. This insight may be very meaningful, but due to the lack of meditative quiescence, it is fleeting, and difficult for the meditator to experience repeatedly.

Just as it is possible to acquire a limited degree of insight without meditative quiescence, so one may experience compassion to some extent without insight. But the most profound spiritual awakening occurs upon the foundation of all three—meditative quiescence, insight, and compassion—and it is for this purpose that one cultivates meditative quiescence.

THE CONDITIONS FOR MEDITATIVE QUIESCENCE

We can begin to stabilize our minds from the beginning of our spiritual practice, while placing our chief emphasis on ethical discipline. By taking out some time each day for the practice of meditative quiescence, we become increasingly aware of how our minds function; and in the process we begin to discover how scattered our minds have been all along. Recognizing this, we may yearn to explore the potentials of the human mind that become apparent only when the awareness is still and lucid.

Six conditions are necessary for the achievement of meditative quiescence. The first of these is a harmonious environment, one in which we feel secure, free from the dangers of war, pollution, contagious disease, and dangerous animals. Food and the other necessities should be easily acquired, and the people with whom we associate should be compatible. The cultivation of meditative quiescence requires a quiet environment, free from the noises of conversation during the day and such noises as the barking of dogs during the night.

The other five conditions are internal qualities. The first of these is having few desires. This is an attitude of being undisturbed by wishes for things we do not have, be it a nicer dwelling, better food, better clothing, and the like.

The third of the six conditions, contentment, complements the second. The attitude of contentment regards present circumstances, whatever they may be, with a sense of satisfaction. When we are contented, we are concerned merely that the physical conditions for our practice are adequate. Once these are taken care of, we are free to focus our attention on our meditation.

The fourth condition of meditative quiescence is limiting our activities. When entering a contemplative retreat for the sake of stabilizing our minds, it is essential to reduce other activities to a bare minimum.

The fifth condition may be the most important of all: pure ethical discipline. This does not mean one is so far advanced one never engages in unwholesome behavior of body, speech, or mind. But it does mean that one is very familiar with the types of behavior to avoid, such as the ten unwholesome deeds; that one continually tries to hold to the ethical principles described previously; and that one takes steps to purify unwholesome actions once they have been committed.

The sixth and final condition is the elimination of compulsive, discursive thinking about desires and other distractions. Many of us find our minds inundated by a torrent of ideas throughout the day. This tendency must be curbed if we are ever to cultivate meditative quiescence. The point of Buddhist meditation is not to stop thinking, for, as we have seen, cultivation of insight clearly requires intelligent use of thought and discrimination. What needs to be stopped is conceptualization that is compulsive, mechanical, and unintelligent, that is, activity that is always fatiguing, usually pointless, and at times seriously harmful.

It is not enough to learn a technique for stabilizing the mind and apply oneself to it with diligence. If these six underlying conditions are not satisfied, meditative quiescence will never arise, regardless of one's determination or perseverance. This is what the renowned Indian sage Atīśa meant in his *Lamp on the Path of Awakening*:

> If the conditions for meditative quiescence are impaired,
> One may meditate intensively

For as long as a thousand years
Without achieving tranquil absorption.

MEDITATIVE OBJECTS FOR STABILIZING THE MIND

In Buddhist practice we can choose among a wide variety of objects for stabilizing the mind. One common method in the Tibetan Buddhist tradition is to focus on an image of the Buddha. First we take a physical object, either a statue or painting of the Buddha, and gaze at it until we are very familiar with its appearance. Then we close our eyes and create a simulation of that image with our imagination.

The actual practice is not the visual one—this is only a preparation—for the point is to stabilize the mind, not the eyes. When we first try to visualize the Buddha, the mental image is bound to be vague and extremely unstable. We may not even be able to get an image at all. I remember teaching this technique many years ago to a group of students in the Swiss Alps. After we had been practicing together for a half hour or so, we took a break to discuss people's initial experiences. One fellow raised his hand, and with some consternation confessed that he was not able to see the Buddha in his mind's eye at all. For awhile his mind was blank; then finally the image of a sea gull flew through the space of his mind!

While the above method has many benefits, it is not ideal for everyone. For it to be effective, one must have a fairly peaceful mind, and it is helpful to have deep faith and reverence for the Buddha. For people of a devotional nature, this practice can be very inspiring, and effective at stabilizing the mind. One's heart is stirred by bringing the Buddha to mind with devotion, and consequently one's enthusiasm for the meditation grows. On the other hand, if one has a very agitated mind and little faith, this and other visualization techniques may very well lead to tension and unhappiness. And these problems may increase the more one practices.

With an agitated, conceptually congested mind, the sheer effort of imagining a visualized object may be too taxing. So if one is engaging in visualization practices, especially during several sessions a day, it is important to be aware of one's level of stress. It is important not to let it get out of hand; for if it does, instead of stabilizing the mind the practice will damage one's nervous system.

Another method that is practiced widely, especially in the Buddhist countries of east and southeast Asia, is focusing one's awareness on the breath. A key attribute of this practice, as opposed to visualization of the Buddha, is that in breath awareness the object of meditation, the breath, is present without our having to imagine it.

Awareness of the breath is practiced in many different ways. Some people focus on the rise and fall of the abdomen during the in- and out-breath. Another technique is to focus on the tactile sensations, from the nostrils down to the abdomen, that are associated with the respiration. In yet another method one focuses on the sensations of the breath passing through the apertures of the nostrils and above the upper lip. All of these are valuable methods, and they can be especially useful for people with highly discursive, imaginative minds. They offer a soothing way to calm the conceptually disturbed mind.

A third method of stabilizing the mind involves directing one's awareness to the mind itself. This is the most subtle of all the techniques mentioned here, and its rewards are great. I shall elaborate on this practice in a moment, but first I would like to discuss some of the themes common to all methods of stabilizing the mind.

Two facets of awareness are instrumental in all the above forms of meditative training. These are mindfulness and vigilance. Mindfulness is a mental factor that allows us to focus upon an object with continuity, without forgetting that object. So, if we are focusing on the sensations of our breath at our nostrils, mindfulness enables us to fasten our attention there continuously. When mindfulness vanishes, the mind slips off its object like a seal off a slick rock. Vigilance is another mental factor, whose function is to check up on the quality of awareness itself. It checks to see if the meditating mind is becoming agitated and scattered, or dull and drowsy. It is the task of vigilance to guard against these extremes.

There are many inner hindrances to stabilizing the mind, but they boil down to the two extremes of excitement and laxity. Excitement is a mental factor that draws our attention away from our intended object. This hindrance is a derivative of desire. If we are meditating and suddenly find ourselves thinking about going to the refrigerator and getting a snack, we can identify this impulse as excitement born from desire. Excitement draws the mind outward. It can easily be stimulated by sound such as that of a car driving by. It compulsively latches onto the sound—a kind of mental hitchhiking—and elaborates on it with a series of images and thoughts.

When the mind is not agitated, it is prone to slipping off to the other extreme of laxity. This mental factor does not distract the attention outward, but brings on a sinking sensation. The mind becomes absorbed in its object without clarity, and drowsiness is bound to follow. At that point the object of the meditation is submerged under waves of lethargy or obliviousness.

The chief antidotes to excitement and laxity are mindfulness and vigilance, and the results of overcoming those hindrances are mental stability and clarity. These are the fruits of the practice.

Meditative stability necessarily implies an underlying ground of relaxation and serenity. The mind is peaceful, and the attention remains where we direct it for as long as we wish. Clarity refers more to the vividness of subjective awareness than to the clarity of the object. When it is present we can detect even the subtle and most fleeting qualities of our object. For example, if we are visualizing the Buddha with clarity, he will appear in our mind's eye in three dimensions and very lifelike. We will be able to see the color of his eyes, the individual folds in his robe. He will appear almost as clearly as if we were seeing him directly with our eyes. Such subjective clarity is instrumental in focusing on the breath as well as on the mind.

All of us have experienced moments when our attention is extremely vivid. This may occur, for example, while driving a car or motorcycle at high speed on a winding road, or when rock-climbing. But when such mental clarity is experienced it is usually combined with a high degree of tension, and the mind is neither serene nor stable. On the other hand, mental stability is a common experience when we are pleasantly tired and we lie down to sleep. But in such cases there is rarely much clarity of awareness.

The challenge of meditative quiescence practice is to cultivate stability integrated with clarity, generating an extraordinarily useful quality of awareness. To bring this about, experienced meditators have found that there must be a sequence of emphases in the practice. First seek a relaxed, wholesome, and cheerful state of mind. On this basis, emphasize stability, and then finally let clarity take priority. The importance of this sequence cannot be overemphasized.

FOCUSING AWARENESS ON THE MIND

Many meditation teachers have made a common observation concerning Western meditators: We *try* so hard! Our efforts in meditation may be sporadic, but when we put our minds to it, we show true grit. This attitude can create a lot of problems. For example, if we are trying to stabilize the mind through the practice of focusing on a Buddha-image, the initial image is bound to be unclear and fleeting. At this stage, meditators are properly advised to be satisfied with a vague object. It is best not to try harder to improve the quality of the image; simply see if we can hold onto it without losing it.

However strongly this may be emphasized, there is a powerful tendency, especially among Westerners, to try harder and harder to create a vivid object, and to hold it with sheer tenacity. This same attitude often prevails among those practicing awareness of the breath. Once again these serious meditators bear down on the object, trying very hard to see it clearly and to hold onto it for dear life. This, after all, is what we have been taught from childhood: "If you want to get ahead, do your best. Try your hardest." Our society often considers these two phrases to be synonymous.

In meditation, however, they are not synonymous. Doing our best in this training does not mean to try our hardest; because, if we are trying our hardest, we are trying too hard. And if we try too hard, we will burn out; and our practice will be sporadic at best, until it fizzles out altogether. Doing our best in meditation means being as skillful as we can at finding the delicate balance between relaxation and exertion.

An especially helpful tool for this is meditation on the mind itself. In this practice we have no clearly delineated, concrete object on which to focus. The mind has no form or location. If we try strenuously to focus our minds on it as our object, it eludes us. The tendency to overexert simply does not work here.

To engage in meditation on the mind, one first finds a suitable posture. Much has been written on this subject, so I shall discuss only some of the major points. It is important to sit in an erect posture, with the spine straight. It is important not to become slouched forward or to tilt to the side or backward. Throughout the meditation session one should keep the body still and relaxed.

At the outset of this or any other Buddhist practice, it is helpful to take refuge. It is also vital to cultivate a good motivation, for this will profoundly influence the nature of the practice. Finally, it is helpful to be cheerful, cherishing this wonderful opportunity to explore the nature of consciousness.

Although the main practice here is awareness of the mind, it is useful to begin with a more tangible object to calm and refine one's awareness. Breath awareness can be perfect for this. We should cultivate a general awareness of the breath coming in and going out. During inhalation, we should simply be aware that this is taking place. During exhalation, we note that the breath is going out. Awareness is allowed to rest calmly in the present, while we breathe in a natural, unforced way.

As we now move on to the main practice, we may follow the counsel of Tilopa, the great Indian Buddhist contemplative: "Do not indulge in thought, but watch the natural awareness."[16] "Natural awareness" has no shape or color, and it has no location. So how can we focus on it? What does it mean "to watch" it?

First of all, our task is to focus our attention on the mind, as opposed to the physical sense fields. One way to do this is to focus our awareness initially on a mental event, such as a thought. This thought could be anything—a word or a phrase—but it is helpful if it is one that does not stimulate either desire or aversion.

One possibility is the phrase: "What is the mind?" The point here is not to speculate on this question, or to try to answer it. Rather, use that thought itself as the object of awareness. Very shortly after having brought that phrase to mind, it is bound to fade out of our consciousness. At that point we keep our awareness right where it is. We have now directed our attention on the mind, and what remains between the vanishing of one thought, and the arising of another, is simply awareness, empty and without obstruction, like space.

An analogy may be helpful. Imagine yourself as a child lying on your back, gazing up into a cloudless sky, and blowing soap bubbles through a plastic ring. As a bubble drifts up into the sky, you watch it rise, and this brings your attention into the sky. While you are looking at the bubble it pops, and you keep your attention right where the bubble had been. Your awareness now lies in empty space.

In the actual meditation practice one focuses initially on the bubble of a thought. When this thought vanishes one does not replace it with some other mental construct. Rather, one stabilizes one's attention in natural awareness, uncontrived, without conceptual elaboration.

This practice is so subtle we may find we become tense in our efforts to do it right. Some people even find the intensity of their concentration impedes their normal respiration—they restrict their breathing for fear it will disturb the delicate equilibrium of their minds. Such tension and constricted respiration can only impair the practice and our health in general. So it is crucial that we engage in the meditation with a sense of physical and mental relaxation.

Starting from relaxation one cultivates meditative stability, resting in natural awareness without being carried away by the turbulence of thoughts or emotions. Finally, it is important to recognize that this practice is not based upon a vague sort of trance or dull absorption; rather, it calls for vivid, clear awareness.

To cultivate these three qualities of relaxation, stability, and clarity, it is usually helpful to keep the meditation sessions relatively short. The chief criterion for determining the length of one's meditation sessions is the quality of one's awareness during the practice. Five minutes of finely conducted meditation is worth more than an hour of low-grade conceptual chatter. Another useful criterion is one's state of mind following meditation. The mind should be refreshed, stable, and clear. If one feels exhausted and dull, one's session was probably too long or of low quality.

PHASES OF THE PRACTICE

Once we have entered into this discipline, it may not be long before we experience short periods—perhaps up to ten seconds or longer—during which we are able to abide in a natural state of awareness, without grasping onto the thoughts and other events that arise in our consciousness. We may well find this delightfully exhilarating, and our minds may then leap upon the experience with glee. But as soon as our minds grasp in this way, the experience will fade. This can be frustrating.

The remedy is to enter into this state of awareness repeatedly. As we become familiar with it, we can then take it in stride, without expectation or anxiety. We learn to just let it be.

As the mind settles in this practice, our awareness of thoughts and other mental events is also bound to change. At times we may no longer sense ourselves thinking, yet a multitude of thoughts and images may arise as simple events. One friend of mine told me that while she was meditating in relative conceptual silence, the thought arose: "Pass the pizza, please." She had not had a pizza for months, nor did she particularly want one at that moment. Thoughts will simply arise, as will entire conversations. When this happens, just let them be.

Do not cling to these thoughts, identify with them, or try to sustain them. But also do not try to suppress them. Simply view them as spontaneous outflows of natural awareness, while centering your attention on the pure, unelaborated awareness from which they arise.

On many occasions we are bound to find ourselves carried away by trains of thought. When we recognize this has happened, we may react with frustration, disappointment, or restlessness.

All such responses are a waste of time. If we find our minds have become agitated, the antidote is to relax more deeply. Relax away the effort that is going into sustaining our conceptual or emotional turbulence. It is best not to silence the mind with a crushing blow of our will. Instead, we may release the effort of grasping onto those mental events. Grasping arises from attachment, and the antidote is simply to let go of this attachment.

On other occasions we may experience mental laxity. Although the mind is not agitated, it may rest in a nebulous blankness. The antidote for this hindrance is to revitalize our awareness by paying closer attention to the practice. The "middle path" here is to invigorate our awareness without agitating it.

The great Indian Buddhist contemplative Saraha says of this practice:

> By releasing the tension that binds the mind,
> One undoubtedly brings about inner freedom.[17]

Tilopa speaks of three phases of the meditation. In the initial stages the onslaught of compulsive ideation is like a stream rushing through a narrow gorge. At this point it may seem that our mind is more out of control, more conceptually turbulent, than it was before we began meditating. But in fact, we are only now realizing how much the mind normally gushes with semiconscious thoughts.

As the mind becomes more quiescent, more stable, the stream of mental activity will become like the Ganges—a broad, quietly flowing river. In the third phase of the practice, the continuum of awareness is like the river flowing into the sea. It is at this point that one recognizes the mind's natural serenity, vividness, transparency, and freshness.

During early stages of practice, we may experience moments of mental quiescence relatively free of conceptualization, and we may wonder whether we are now ascertaining natural awareness. Most likely we are not. Our mind at this point is probably still too gross and unclear for such a realization. Patience is needed to persist in the practice, without expectation or fear, until gradually the essential qualities of awareness become apparent. When we ascertain the simple clarity and knowing qualities of the awareness, we are well established in the practice. We can then proceed to the attainment of meditative quiescence focused on the mind.

THE ATTAINMENT OF MEDITATIVE QUIESCENCE

In Buddhist practice the achievement of meditative quiescence is clearly defined. As a result of the practice outlined above, one eventually experiences natural awareness, and the duration of this experience gradually increases. Eventually we no longer become distracted or agitated. At this point the emphasis of the practice should be on cultivating clarity. For the mind, even after it has become well stabilized, can still easily slip into laxity.

When we finally attain meditative quiescence, we are free of even the subtle forms of excitement and laxity. During the early phases of practice, considerable degrees of effort are required, but as we progress, more and more subtle effort suffices. Gradually the meditation becomes effortless, and we can sustain each session for hours on end.

Benefits from this practice are also evident between formal meditation sessions. The mind becomes so refined and stable that it is very difficult for mental distortions to arise. And even when they do occur, they are relatively impotent and short-lived. Through the attainment of meditative quiescence, the mind is brought to such a state of heightened sanity it is very difficult for these afflictions to thrive. In addition, one will experience an unprecedented quality of inner well-being that arises from the balance and health of the mind. Due to the shifts in the energies experienced in the body (closely related to the nervous system), one will experience a delightful sense of physical lightness and buoyancy.

The attainment of meditative quiescence is also said to be a fertile basis from which to cultivate various types of heightened awareness such as clairvoyance. When cultivated and employed with wisdom and compassion, these can be very useful. Otherwise, they are simply a distraction at best, and may be a real source of danger.

In Buddhist practice the chief purpose of attaining meditative quiescence is to use this refined state of awareness for investigating the nature of reality. Meditative quiescence by itself is a temporary achievement that can easily be lost, especially if one becomes immersed once again in a hectic, turbulent way of life. Only by using the mind that has been trained in meditative quiescence is it possible to gain the depth of insight needed to utterly uproot the fundamental distortions of the mind, which are the root of suffering.

In the meantime, the cultivation of meditative quiescence is something that brings us greater sanity, serenity, stability, and clarity. This is bound to aid us in all the pursuits worthy of our precious lives.

10

LOVING KINDNESS

The cultivation of loving kindness is ideally suited for the bustling world we live in. It generates a quality of mind that wishes for the well-being of others, and at the same time it profoundly enhances our ability to attain well-being in our own lives. Instead of focusing on a poised state of mental peace, it is a discursive meditation that penetrates deeper into the root causes of our dissatisfactions and transforms them. It offers us a way to understand the distortions of the mind, and a way to defuse these distortions by means of an attitude of loving kindness that springs from the essential purity of our minds.

Loving kindness can be seen as a very potent remedy for the most malignant of the mental distortions: hatred. Having dissolved that, loving kindness is also capable of countering the other distortions as well. Many people believe in the value of anger, arguing that without its forcefulness we are less than fully human. Putting that question aside for the time being, I think we can all agree that hatred is quite another matter. Hatred is simply an expression of malice. Hatred breeds contempt, hostility, resentment, and aggression. And experience has proven that those who become absorbed in hatred eventually inflict tremendous pain and destruction on themselves, as well as on the sentient beings around them.

LOVING KINDNESS TOWARD ONESELF

Loving kindness practice traditionally starts with oneself, and then proceeds, step-by-step, to an attitude of loving kindness toward all sentient beings in the universe.

To develop an attitude of loving kindness, first we must develop a truly loving attitude toward ourselves, compassionately understanding our own desire to be happy and to avoid suffering. As part of that, we must understand the nature of our own ignorance that thwarts this desire for happiness and instead brings suffering. This done, we will have taken an essential first step toward developing loving kindness toward all beings.

To bring this closer to our own lives, let us consider self-contempt. While few of us may actually experience overt self-hatred, it is fairly common for people in our society to struggle with self-contempt, a feeling of impatience and intolerance toward ourselves. For many, this culminates in the feeling that we are not worthy of love from someone else or even from ourselves. Seen in this light, self-contempt is obviously a poor basis for the cultivation of loving kindness.

Let us turn to a fifth-century text, Buddhaghosa's *The Path of Purification*, that offers us a set of wishes that will help us develop loving kindness toward ourselves:

> May I be free of enmity,
> May I be free of afflictions.
> May I be free of anxiety,
> And may I live happily. [18]

The first, "May I be free of enmity," is a wish that we may develop friendliness devoid of animosity. In the second wish, "May I be free of afflictions," we can understand afflictions as referring to both physical pain and mental distress, sadness, grief, and discontent. We may also look more deeply to the very source of all distress, namely the mental defilements such as ignorance, greed, and hatred, from which all afflictions arise. The wish for freedom from anxiety needs no explanation. And the last line, "May I live happily," refers especially to a quality of well-being that arises from a wholesome mind.

DEVELOPING THE PRACTICE

In the cultivation of loving kindness one first begins with oneself as an example, and then extends this attitude toward others by simple analogy. However, although the cultivation of loving kindness toward oneself is an important first step, it is not the full practice. Starting from the foundation of loving kindness toward oneself, this practice develops loving kindness toward others in three stages of increasing difficulty.

The first of these entails bringing to mind a person toward whom we already feel affection. We first reflect upon that person's good qualities, which may be the basis for holding that person so dear. We then reflect that this person, like ourselves, desires happiness and wishes to be free from suffering and anxiety. We then cultivate the wish, "May you be free of enmity," realizing that if that person does experience enmity, it does not spring from his or her essential nature any more than our own feelings of enmity are expressions of our own essential nature. We continue: "May you be free of afflictions," mental and physical, just as we wish for ourselves. And then we conclude with the wishes, "May you be free of anxiety," and "May you live happily."

The next step is to develop loving kindness toward someone we know quite well, but toward whom we feel relative indifference. Now we meditate on this person in the same way we meditated on the loved one. First we consider the fact that this person has the same essential desires as ourselves, the same yearning for happiness, the same hope to avoid suffering. Then we proceed the same as before, wishing that this person be happy, with a life free of enmity, afflictions, and anxiety.

The most difficult, however, is the final stage, that involves developing loving kindness toward a person towards whom we feel animosity. This may be a person whom we perceive as having done us a lot of harm, or perhaps someone whom we simply find offensive.

Most people's response to someone they dislike is to regard this person as an object that is intrinsically dislikeable. But the point of this practice is to penetrate this conception of object-ness and truly realize that this dislikeable person is after all a sentient being.

Again, we must reflect that this person, like ourselves, is seeking happiness and trying to be free of suffering, although perhaps in a very confused way. And we may realize that much of what makes this person dislikeable is the fact that his or her mental afflictions are so strong that they dominate the person's attempts to find happiness. Instead of leading to causes for contentment, they only create more unhappiness for that person, as they do for ourselves.

This realization is the root of compassion. And from that perspective, we may direct our minds to that person with the sincere wish that he or she be happy and free of enmity, afflictions, and anxiety.

THE REALIZATION OF IMPERMANENCE AS AN ANTIDOTE

Insight into impermanence can aid in the cultivation of loving kindness. In essence, realization of impermanence is a natural result of looking into the nature of events, both physical and mental. As we have mentioned, the mind is in a state of constant flux. Not even awareness itself is static and immutable. Moments of awareness are conditioned by ever-changing outer and inner conditions.

Forgetting this leads to a distorted sense of permanence in human behavior. We can check this out with our own experience. When we are really feeling resentment toward another person, we may think of the unkind things that person did as if that person were a veritable wellspring of unkindness. In our resentment we ignore that person's impermanent nature, concluding that the person's actions and behavior are merely expressions of something that is at the core unwholesome.

But in fact, said the Buddha, such an intrinsically unwholesome person does not exist. What we see in ourselves and others are expressions of habitual propensities. Nearly everyone has the seeds for hatred, which have their origins in some prior event or action. Even though those propensities may not be activated at one moment, they may be brought to life later by certain events, or even by recollections.

An emotion many of us may find very satisfying is righteous indignation, righteous hatred. But how satisfying is it really? One may have the feeling that righteous hatred is justified. It may be clear the person one is angry at has acted in an obnoxious, thoughtless way. That person may have harmed one in certain ways, through abuse, slander, or dishonesty. But the truth is, he cannot reach into one's mind. If one's mind is hurt, it is because the mind is still subject to mental affliction. To compound the pain by nurturing resentment simply does not make sense.

To decide to hate someone is like taking a little hurt and creating from it a much larger hurt that will sit inside us and fester. "Righteous hatred" is in the same category as "righteous cancer" or "righteous tuberculosis." All of them are absurd concepts.

One of the simplest practices of loving kindness is to remember those beings who have manifested loving kindness in their own lives, whether it be the Buddha, or some other holy being. From the example of these great beings we can learn about forgiveness, as an expression of loving kindness. We may know of some very great beings who were harmed greatly but responded with forgiveness.

The Buddha spoke at length about the cultivation of loving kindness, and the benefits from it. While loving kindness is limitless, both hatred and anger do have limits. Describing the eleven virtues of loving kindness, the Buddha said:

> One sleeps in comfort, wakes in comfort, and dreams no
> evil dreams. One is dear to human beings, one is dear to
> nonhuman beings, deities guard one, fire and poison and
> weapons do not affect one. One's mind is easily concentrated,
> the expression of one's face is serene, one dies unconfused.

If one penetrates no higher, one will be reborn in
the Brahma world.[19]

There is yet another loving kindness practice that is very simple,
and very profound. It involves a deep investigation into the precise
nature of the object of our hatred. First we must ask ourselves, "Is it
the person's body we are angry at." We find that we must answer in
the negative. "We do not hate the person's body, we hate the person." The next question is, "Do we hate the person's mind?" As we
contemplate the nature of the mind, we find that it is not just one
substance we can hate, but a myriad of related events. The minds of
all of us include collections of joys and sorrows, all in continuous
flux. Although we may conclude that we hate the present state of
this person's mind, that state does not exist on its own, but is conditioned by other events, and is subject to change.

We can ask ourselves: "Where is the person we hate so much?
Where is the intrinsically bad person we believe stands outside of
this body, and outside this fluctuating mind?" As we investigate
more deeply, we find there is no such person: there is no intrinsic,
personal self, nobody that stands apart from the constant fluctua-
tion of mental and physical events.

The goal is to look at everyone as the Buddha would: with loving kindness for ourselves, for the ones we love, for those who are
neither friend nor foe, and for those who feel animosity toward us.
In short, the goal of loving kindness practice is a deep realization
that all sentient beings are all equally deserving of our affection.

11

FOUR APPLICATIONS OF MINDFULNESS

THE ROLE OF INSIGHT

To uproot ignorance, the fundamental affliction of the mind, one needs insight into the nature of reality. In Sanskrit this is called *vipaśyanā*. Its basis is a stable mind, and the basis of that is moral discipline.

There are many forms of vipaśyanā, or insight meditation. Here we will explore a discipline known as the close application of mindfulness (known as *satipaṭṭhāna* in the Pali language). One can fruitfully engage in this practice without having attained meditative quiescence, but in order for this practice to be fully effective, one does need to have a stable mind. Without a stable mind one may gain some flashes of insight from one's satipaṭṭhāna practice, but these will not have the full transformative effect that occurs with meditative quiescence.

If we are to overcome the ignorance that lies at the root of other mental distortions, we need to enter into the experience of insight again and again, saturating the mind. As we become more experienced with insight into the true nature of reality, our ignorance will be swept away just as darkness is swept away by light.

MINDFULNESS OF THE BODY

The path of satipaṭṭhāna, or close application of mindfulness, is one of the great paths to enlightenment. But unhappily, some adherents of this path believe it is the only way, and present it as if it were so. But in fact, that is not what the Buddha said. The word he used to describe this mindfulness training is *ekayāna; eka* means "one," *yāna* means "way." Consequently, ekayāna means "one way," not that it is "the only way."

This question is discussed in early Theravāda commentaries to the Buddha's discourse on the close application of mindfulness. Various interpretations of the word ekayāna are given. One interpretation is that it goes "only to nirvāṇa." Another interpretation is that it is a "solitary path" that must be trodden by oneself, not by anyone else. Neither the Buddha, nor these authoritative commentaries, indicate it is the "sole way" to liberation.[20]

The four applications of mindfulness concern mindfulness directed to four types of phenomena: the body, feelings, the mind, and other events, both mental and physical. Like most Buddhist practices, mindfulness training starts with the grossest, easiest object of practice, and then progresses to the most subtle, which is also the most difficult. In this case among the four objects we are going to consider—the body, the feelings, the mind, and other events—the body is the grossest. It makes good sense to start out with practices that are more basic, and objects of meditation that are relatively gross, for when we begin practice our minds are at their grossest. As we progress our minds become more refined, more subtle, and we are in a position to attend to objects that are more subtle.

The major theme in all four mindfulness practices is to distinguish more and more clearly between our conceptual projections upon reality, and what reality itself presents to us. This turns out to be a very formidable project. As we start, we find the role of our conceptual projection is deeply ingrained, much of it occurring either unconsciously or only semiconsciously.

Because conceptualization is largely semiconscious, we usually are not aware that this compulsive and semiconscious interpretation is taking place. Instead, we tend to assume we are not projecting anything on reality at all, and that our basic sense of things is valid. There can be a lot of delusion in that. The application of mindfulness takes a mental scalpel created by quieting the mind, and uses this scalpel to slice through conceptual projections. In doing so we penetrate into the essential reality that is present in the absence of conceptual projections.

As the Buddha taught this practice, he said to first sit down and simply follow the breath. One first gets into a comfortable position, brings one's awareness into the present, and stabilizes it by following the in-breath and the out-breath. The emphasis here, as it often is in Buddhism, is on developing a fine tool. Just as in science one must develop finely honed tools to make reliable, precise measurements, so in contemplative practice one must hone the tool of one's awareness to understand the nature of reality.

The practice starts quite simply, with posture. The Buddha spoke of four simple postures we already engage in: sitting, standing, walking and lying down. The point of applying mindfulness to these is to engage our awareness and direct it toward our posture. It is often the case that whatever we are doing, be it sitting, walking, standing, or lying, the mind is frequently disengaged from the immediate reality and is instead absorbed in compulsive conceptualization about the future or past. While we are walking, we think about arriving, and when we arrive, we think about leaving. When we are eating, we think about the dishes, and as we do the dishes, we think about watching television.

This is a weird way to run a mind. We are not connected with the present situation, but we are always thinking about something else. Too often we are consumed with anxiety and cravings, regrets about the past and anticipation for the future, completely missing the crisp simplicity of the moment.

A very important mindfulness practice is based on one of the most fundamental human activities: walking. We are accustomed to walking along busily, thinking ahead to where we are going and forgetting where we are. Our eyes wander everywhere, and our minds are like eggs being scrambled, flipping from one thing to another. But another possibility is to pull our awareness out of this mesh of compulsive, exhausting ideation, and instead bring it to the soles of our feet. This allows us to be aware of the feet rising and falling, to be aware of the contact with the earth.

It can help to slow the walking down. In this practice one walks very slowly and deliberately, paying close attention to each moment. First the foot is rising, rising, rising; then, ever so slowly, it is placing, placing, placing. One is aware of the tactile sensations of the body, and the sensations of the soles of the feet on the ground. It grounds one, literally and metaphorically. It brings one's awareness into the present.

This may sound boring, but that is only because we are so used to not being in the present. If we start doing this well, if we really start calming the mind and bringing it into the body, we find it turns out to be fascinating.

Imagine you are sitting totally motionless, and then, when you are firmly in the present, you do something that is quite extraordinary—you raise your hand! As you learn to do this mindfully, you find this simple activity has many parts. There is an intention, a mental event, and somehow this results in the hand moving, a physical event. How do they connect? How did this happen? It becomes an absorbing process.

One central aspect of this practice is mindfulness, which in this context means maintaining a continuity of awareness of one's chosen object. Another is vigilance, which refers here to a keen and intelligent examination of events.

THE NATURE OF THE SELF

Now let us consider how this finely honed tool, this mindfulness, can generate insight into the essential question of the spiritual path: What is the nature of the self?

A famous commentary by Buddhaghosa sheds light on this. Speaking of physical motion, he says:

A living being goes, a living being stands...but truly,
there is no living being going or standing. This talk of
a living being going and standing is similar to speech in
the following way: A cart goes, a cart stands.[21]

The point he is raising here is exactly what makes the cart go or
not go, the living being go or not go. What is the source of their
motion, or, looked at on a deeper level, what is the source of the
volition that makes them move? What is this self from which
motion apparently comes?

It is evidently true that the cart is moved by something, perhaps a
bull, a harness attaching the bull to the cart, maybe a driver to direct
the bull. On a subtler level, the event of a living being standing and
going also has causes and conditions. In fact, movement takes place as
a result of complex interactions of external and internal events.
Nowhere does one find an autonomous self that takes charge and
says, "I am going to move the hand," and then it moves. This, of
course, is counter to our gut sense of things, our inherent sense that
each of us is a self-sufficient "I" who is in charge of our behavior.
However, through mindfulness practice we can develop great insight
into the nature of selflessness or the noninherent existence of the "I."

To do this, we simply start to investigate. Starting from the
gross and moving to the subtle, we focus the finely tuned tool of
awareness on the components of action, and analyze them. Gazing
upon the physical and mental causes of motion, we find that nowhere
is there any evidence of an inherent "my-ness," or of an essential self,
anywhere in the body, the flesh, the bones, or the marrow.

MINDFULNESS OF FEELINGS

The feelings are the second object for the application of mindfulness.
A step more subtle than identification with the body, identification
with feelings can take us on a roller coaster of feeling good and feeling bad that can be very difficult to penetrate.

While the word "feelings" is used in many ways in English, referring to emotions as well as tactile sensations, in Buddhism it has a
more restricted meaning, captured in the Sanskrit word *vedanā*. This
word refers simply to the feelings of pleasure, pain, and indifference,
with which we can so easily identify ourselves. This is a very powerful point, because if we identify with our body, certainly it is equally
true we identify with our feelings.

When unhappiness arises, we respond with the thoughts, "I am
unhappy, I am depressed, I am so discouraged." And when happiness
arises it is much the same: "I am happy! I'm feeling great!" The key is
that none of these feelings are in fact "I." Like the movements of the
body they arise from causes and conditions, and these are ever-changing.

The feelings we identify with are rooted in propensities unique
to ourselves. If someone praises me in a way that fits my propensities I will feel happy, while someone else's praise might cause me
to react indifferently. On the negative side, the same goes for blame
and feelings of sadness. In either case, the feelings are simply one
instant within a causal matrix of events.

The problem with feelings is that we identify with them so
strongly. We almost never cut through the conceptual overlay that
causes us to regard certain feelings as inherently "our feelings." In
fact, feelings are inherently no one's. All that is taking place is the arising and passing of feelings, brought about by causes and conditions.

The Buddha spoke of several qualities of feelings, one of the
most important being their impermanence. Despair, for example,
which can seem so leaden, is in fact an emotion that is in constant
flux. Even the heaviest feelings are constantly changing, but this is
very difficult to recognize. Identification with depression obscures
the fluctuations that are taking place from one moment to the next,
replacing them instead with a sense of a homogeneous continuity.

Sometimes things go well, we feel great, and we think, "Now
my troubles are over, that was the last hurdle." Our conceptual
mind plays another trick on us, and we think, "As it is now, so it

must be forever." The same applies to the downside, of course. Sorrow sets in, and the mind becomes negative: "I am really a failure, I will be a failure next year, in fact my whole life is a failure." Again, these feelings are arising in the moment, and the mind is fixing on that moment in a deluded way.

The problem with attachment to feelings, especially if they are hinged upon pleasurable external stimuli, is that everything around us is constantly changing, most of it out of our control. We try to manipulate and control our immediate environment, but even our own body is to a significant degree beyond our control. Our mind, too, is often out of our control.

Grasping onto pleasurable feelings is not bad in the sense of being evil, but rather in the sense that it is not effective. As the well-known Burmese Buddhist teacher Goenka once said, "Grasping at things can yield only one of two results: either the thing you are grasping at disappears, or you yourself disappear. It is only a matter of which occurs first."

MINDFULNESS OF THE MIND

Mindfulness of the mind is quite different from the practice of meditative quiescence focused on the mind, which was described in Chapter Nine. That practice is a penetrating and focused look at pure awareness, but this mindfulness practice is instead a meditation on the ways in which the mind works.

Mindfulness of the mind is not a practice to develop stability, but is instead an insight practice. The object of meditation here is the mental states rather than awareness itself.

An important part of this practice is investigating the mind dominated by the three poisons we discussed: ignorance, hatred, and attachment. In this practice the meditator notes and investigates these mind states, with special emphasis on the "tone" of the mind as these states arise.

In normal life, we tend to do quite the opposite. When the mind manifests anger, for instance, we immediately identify with it. I spill a glass of water on my trousers, and without thinking I focus out there on an object, either the glass itself or the person who bumped my elbow and made me spill it, and I become angry. I am identifying with the anger. And if someone should ask me how I am doing, I will say, "I am angry." I have identified with a mental event that is not I.

Mental events like anger arise out of our own propensities for anger, which are activated by external events. On that level we have no choice, because if we have those propensities and the necessary conditions arise, we will experience anger. We may forget everything we have heard about mindfulness, and the next time anger arises we will simply identify with it. We focus on the object of anger, we think about it, and we act upon it. Everything is predictable and mechanical.

By introducing mindfulness, however, the possibility of choice is presented. We do not identify with the event, but we attend to it mindfully. Considering anger again, we are now faced with a meaningful choice. Being aware, "Aha, the event of anger has arisen again," we can choose between identifying with the event or being mindful. Do we want to act upon the anger, or do we simply want to observe it? If we have mindfulness we are presented with the choice. We have an option.

Recall Śāntideva's suggestion that when our minds are dominated by the mental distortions, such as jealousy, contempt, resentment, and sarcasm, we should remain as a block of wood. This does not mean that we should unintelligently suppress or repress those negative feelings. This will only make us sick; it is bad for the heart, for the digestion, for the blood pressure.

The Buddhist alternative is mindfulness. By exercising mindfulness, we may become clearly aware in the presence of harmful mental events taking place. And by being mindful of them, we are not perpetuating them. Anger and other negativities must be "fed" to survive. Let us say I am angry at Harry, and I want to feed that anger, so I think of all the nasty things he has done. And if this is not enough, I can think of all the nasty things he would do if he had a chance. This keeps the anger going; it can feed the anger for decades.

When Śāntideva suggested we remain as a block of wood when afflictions arise, what he meant was not to feed the anger. Rather than feeding it, we may direct our awareness to the anger itself and be mindful of it so that we do not allow it to dominate our speech or physical behavior.

When the mind is swayed by a mental distortion it is dysfunctional, like a sprained wrist. When the mind is dysfunctional, we can let it heal a bit, and then act. This can prevent a lot of problems, and can solve others that need not have arisen in the first place.

MINDFULNESS OF EVENTS

The most subtle of these practices, mindfulness of events, encompasses all we have discussed above. We have proceeded here from the gross to the subtle, from mindfulness of the body, to mindfulness of feelings, to mindfulness of mind states. In each of these practices the emphasis has been on close inspection, a direct application of attention on the theme we started out with.

That theme, you may recall, is whether or not there is a substantial self, or ego, to be found within the body, feelings, or mind states. We start with the body, trying to see if there is a substantial ego, a self, hidden in there somewhere. Then we move on to the feelings, because we do tend to identify with them at least as strongly. As we inspect the feelings moment by moment, the questions are much the same: Is there an "I" in there? Is there an agent? Is there an entity that feels, apart from the feelings themselves? We investigate and we investigate, and all we see are mere events, arising and passing.

Close inspection of the third stage, the mind, yields a similar result. By directing the awareness to the nature of the mind itself, the mental events, and the mind with its mental distortions, we find the same thing; that is, mental events arising and passing. Even awareness itself is arising and passing, without any personal identity. Awareness has no intrinsic identity. It is just awareness. And mental distortions have no identity either; they are just mental distortions.

At this point a critical observer may protest, saying, "If you want to find the self, investigate who is doing the looking. It is futile to look for a flashlight in a pitch-black room with that same flashlight, and in the same way, the fact that you cannot find the self in the body, feelings, or mind does not mean it is not there. There is a self and that self is doing the looking and the meditating."

Buddhism responds to this by asserting that while we are born with a natural, unlearned sense of intrinsic self, that does not mean such a self actually exists. We think, "I will, therefore I am. I intend, therefore I am. I meditate, therefore I am." This sense that things flow from me, that thoughts flow from me, is associated with this inborn sense of personal identity.

We look at someone who is repugnant, and we somehow feel it is the person himself gushing forth repugnance. We feel there is a source for all the qualities we identify a person with, and that the source is the person behind the scene, the self, the "I" that is in charge.

We have an inborn sense there is an autonomous self in control. This self, we believe, is the one making things coherent, making any one of us a human being. And without this self, one might think, everything would fall apart and there would be no person at all.

This can be checked, not by looking for the self, but by observing the interactions of the body, feelings, mental states, and other events. It is like a company where the workers are told the factory would shut down if there were no outside owner overseeing them. As a worker one might believe that, until one starts analyzing the individual connections. And then one can see that the interrelationships among the workers continue to function without the owner, and the company continues to operate. The workers, acting together, manage themselves.

When the mind is stabilized, it is possible to withdraw the sense of an ego controlling the body and mind, and simply enter a witnessing mode of awareness. And in that state we find that mental and physical behavior occurs only in relation to other events; it does not need a controlling ego. All the elements of the body-mind system interact as coherent dependently related events and, in fact, there is no room for an autonomous ego at all.

Mindfulness covers a wide range of events, generating insight about how all of them interrelate. The events we investigate include all the physical events of the body and things external to the body; all the feelings and mental formations, and finally, awareness itself. And the revelation from all of this is that there is no autonomous self coordinating these events, but rather a complex set of interrelationships that operate on their own, without a single, external manager.

Again and again the Buddha said, when discussing this, that we should check this out with our own experience. We should gain insight, and then apply this in our experience with others. Sometimes we can do this perceptually, by observing other people's behavior. But when we are considering mind states this is not normally possible, and so we must inferentially extrapolate from our own experience. This is done by reflecting, "As this arises in my experience, so it likely occurs in the experience of others." The process is similar to the one we explored in the practice of loving kindness, where we started by generating loving kindness toward ourselves, then extended that to other beings.

THREE THEMES

There are three themes the Buddha emphasized strongly for these insight practices: impermanence, dissatisfaction (suffering), and identitylessness.

Impermanence is understood only when we saturate our minds with the fluctuating, transient nature of all conditioned phenomena. Why is this so important? It is crucial because so much of what we do and think in life is founded on quite the opposite premise: that things are static, and can be made to stay the way we want them to be.

A key problem in life is that we tend to reify things, making them seem permanent and stable when in fact they are not. We enter into relationships, we acquire things, and we say, "Ah, here lies my happiness." In doing this, we suppress the transient nature of the experienced world. It is one thing to know this intellectually, but quite another to experience it moment by moment, and to adapt our way of life accordingly. By recognizing our attachments to these events, to these people, we can cut through this false sense of permanence and replace it with a deeper insight into reality.

Dissatisfaction (suffering) is the second theme, also called *duḥkha*. The emphasis here, as discussed previously, is to recognize the reality of our lives. A common mistake is to hinge our entire well-being on pleasant stimuli from the outside—on a house, a family, a spouse, a child—all situations that are subject to change at every moment. We grasp at these things urgently as if they will support us, but they will not. Instead they will inevitably change, and if we invest our well-being in them with attachment, we will experience nothing but anxiety as those changes affect us. That is suffering, not because the situation is wrong, but because we seek an enduring basis for well-being in events that do not endure.

The last is identitylessness, the lack of an intrinsic self. This is crucial because the opposite, grasping at an intrinsic self, is the confusion posited as the fundamental mental distortion, the root from which all other afflictions arise.

All of the above are fundamental Buddhist teachings. Their major emphasis is on healing the individual, on bringing about greater sanity for the individual. Let us now explore in the following chapters the Mahāyāna practices that develop these themes, opening deeper dimensions for insight through the integration of wisdom and compassion.

12

INDIVIDUAL AND UNIVERSAL VEHICLES
OF BUDDHISM

THE INDIVIDUAL VEHICLE

Tibetan Buddhism identifies three orientations of an individual toward spiritual practice. The first of these is that of a person of "small capacity," whose perspective toward Dharma is essentially one of maintaining or enhancing one's worldly sense of well-being. Taking into account one's future lives, which reach to the distant future, a person of small capacity places a higher priority on sowing the seeds for felicity in the hereafter than on the eight worldly concerns of this life alone. With this motivation, one applies oneself to virtue and seeks to avoid nonvirtue.

A person of medium capacity investigates more deeply the origin and nature of suffering. He considers how the mind is afflicted with such things as craving, hostility, and confusion, and the type of lifestyle these afflictions generate. Bearing in mind the three characteristics of impermanence, suffering, and identitylessness, a person of medium capacity is concerned with more than coping or maintaining his present degree of well-being. Instead, motivated by an emergent attitude, he aspires to attain final liberation from suffering and its source. This Buddhist practice is called the "individual vehicle," for its practices are all matters of individual effort, and the consequences of those practices manifest in the individual and for the individual.

According to Buddhism, the individual path leads to an end of the cycle of rebirth. Many Buddhists regard this as a suitable ultimate goal of spiritual practice. But others may ask, "What is the point? Does it make sense to have lived innumerable lifetimes since beginningless time, only to find that the culmination of all that is to stop?" Or again: "What happened to the Buddha himself when he attained spiritual awakening under the Bodhi tree?" On more than one occasion when the Buddha was asked about these larger metaphysical questions, he would not reply. When asked if the universe has a beginning or not, he would not reply. When asked to explain his silence on these subjects, he gave the parable of a man shot with a poisoned arrow. When a man is dying of poison, the Buddha said, it is pointless to ask where the arrow came from or who shot it. The key issue is pulling it out.

So the Buddha's first message was to deal with immediate and practical things—the alleviation of suffering and mental distortions—before wading into the sea of metaphysics. It is a reasonable system, requiring no leap of faith and focusing on individual effort. And many people say, "This alone was what the Buddha taught. He refused to discuss metaphysical issues."

But others say this is not the whole answer since Buddhism also has room for asking the great questions about the meaning of life. And it is here that we cross a threshold, shifting from the middling perspective to what is commonly called *Mahāyāna*, or the great vehicle.

THE UNIVERSAL VEHICLE

Another translation of Mahāyāna is the *universal vehicle.* While the individual vehicle is focused on the individual, the universal vehicle is focused on the entire universe of sentient beings. The motivation of a person of great capacity who adopts this vehicle, is not just to attain one's own liberation, but to strive for the highest possible spiritual awakening for the benefit of all beings.

The historical origins of Buddhism are helpful in explaining the relationship between the individual and the universal vehicles. The essential teachings of the individual vehicle are contained in what is known as the Pali Canon, which are the teachings of the Buddha recorded in the Pali language. These teachings are fundamental, and they are almost exclusively focused on the individual path.

So where do the Mahāyāna teachings come from? Traditional advocates of Mahāyāna tradition say they also come from the Buddha. In addition to teaching how to become an arhat through the attainment of nirvāṇa, as explained in the Pali Canon, the Buddha also taught elaborately on how to become a Buddha like himself. The Tibetan Buddhist point of view is that during the Buddha's lifetime the time was not ripe for these teachings to be taught to the general public. Because of this, tradition says, the teachings were preserved very secretly and passed down orally for hundreds of years before they were even written down. It was not until about the first century of the Christian era that the Mahāyāna teachings started to be disseminated publicly. Once they were made public they spread rapidly as far west as Afghanistan and eastward across China, eventually to Korea and Japan as well as to parts of Southeast Asia.

How is it that the Buddha could give two sets of teachings, but one of those sets was kept hidden for hundreds of years? The Mahāyāna school has a rather elegant explanation for this, one that gets to the very root of an essential distinction between the schools.

The Buddha's discourses on the theme of the "Perfection of Wisdom" are a striking example of the way the Mahāyāna point of view seems to bend our conventional assumptions about the nature of reality. The records of these teachings say that hundreds of thousands of bodhisattvas, arhats, monks, lay people, devas, and other beings all convened on Vultures' Peak, an actual place in India, to listen to the Buddha teach.

But the problem is, as the Dalai Lama points out in his book *Transcendent Wisdom*, Vultures' Peak is physically too small to have accommodated all those beings. What does this mean? Did the peak somehow erode in the short period of 2,500 years? That seems unlikely. Instead, traditional Mahāyānists believe that even though many beings were present when the Buddha taught, some of them existed in different realms, or dimensions, allowing all of them to be present simultaneously. And what is more, different groups simultaneously heard different teachings.

This latter point is based on the concept of karma, the idea that different entities brought with them to Vultures' Peak different karmic imprints from previous lives. And these determined their abilities to hear the Buddha's teachings in varying ways.

From this point of view, what each entity was hearing was not a matter of what the Buddha, as an objective entity, on an objective hill, was teaching. Instead, what each was hearing and experiencing was inextricably related to subjective conditions each had brought to the event.

If we look again at the teachings of the individual vehicle, we can begin to put this in context. Remember that what is being challenged in the individual vehicle is our basic assumption about the nature of the self, that is, whether or not we intrinsically exist as immutable ego-substances. These teachings also question our assumptions about physical phenomena, pointing out, for instance, that all things are in flux and are only events. But a more encompassing issue, whether or not the world exists intrinsically, receives far more attention in the Mahāyāna teachings.

Mahāyāna challenges our natural assumption that our physical world, the one we experience through our senses, exists independently of our sensory perceptions and conceptions. Working with an integrated philosophical and contemplative approach, it concludes that the world we perceive does not exist independently of our perception of it; nor does the world as we conceive it exist independently of our concepts. Instead, reality is actually an integrated system of experienced events, including both the experiences of individuals and a larger sense of the collective experience of many people.

Applying this to the issues raised by the Buddha's talk at Vultures' Peak, we begin to see some answers emerge. From this point of view, the event of his teachings was not a matter of a speaker uttering objective words to static listeners, but rather a system of speaking and listening that were inextricably intertwined. And because the beings listening to the Buddha existed on profoundly different spiritual levels, the event perceived by one group was very different from the event perceived by another.

With all this in mind, we can ask again: "What is the nature of reality?" The answer is that the reality we experience is contingent upon our perceptual and conceptual faculties. Although phenomena appear to exist in themselves, utterly independent from percepts and concepts, this is not how they exist.

This is a major departure from the assumptions of the individual vehicle, or any realist system. One form of realism says that reality exists as it appears. We can describe it and our description is either wrong or right, depending on whether or not that description accurately corresponds to objective reality. But with the assertion that the reality we experience only exists in dependence upon our conceptions, then what does a "correct description" mean? And if an unmediated experience of ultimate reality is entirely beyond our conception, the idea of a correct description of ultimate reality becomes deeply problematic.

Now we can begin to understand the Buddha as giving many different teachings to many different individuals. All of those teachings used conceptual tools to guide the listeners toward an experience of reality that cannot be grasped with concepts.

We may have a deep realization of something, but that does not mean we can put it into words that can give another person the same realization. This is also true of experience more generally. For example, if a person has never tasted anything sweet, it is pointless to try to describe the taste of chocolate to him. As listeners, all we can do with language is to understand it in terms of our own experience. We cannot adopt the perspective of the speaker.

One important question that is dealt with differently in the individual and universal vehicles of Buddhism is: What happens to a Buddha after death; or in a larger sense, what is a Buddha? According to the individual vehicle, the Buddha was an enlightened man who died, never to be reborn in the cycle of existence. From the Mahāyāna perspective the question of who the Buddha was is part of a much larger view. Explaining this will require three Sanskrit words.

The first, *dharmakāya*, is literally translated as the "body of truth," *dharma* meaning *truth* and *kāya* meaning *body*. It might also be translated as the *spiritual body* of the Buddha. In the Mahāyāna tradition, the consciousness of a Buddha is said to be a transcendent consciousness pervading all of reality simultaneously. It is aware of all reality through time and space, it is everywhere present, and it has inexhaustible, inexpressible power.

Forms are produced by the dharmakāya, as the infinite power of Buddha mind manifests. One of the manifestations of the Buddha mind is called *sambhogakāya*, or *fulfilled body*, depicted as a humanlike form that is so subtle only very highly realized beings can perceive it. Such beings include Buddhas and ārya-bodhisattvas, or bodhisattvas who have attained a direct realization of ultimate truth. To ordinary beings like us, sambhogakāyas are inaccessible.

From sambhogakāya there comes a further emanation, *nirmāṇakāya*, or *emanated body*. These grosser forms can appear in our world. And from the Mahāyāna perspective it is said that the historical Buddha was a nirmāṇakāya, a physical manifestation of the dharmakāya.

When we consider ideas like these, we are moving beyond the parallels with psychology that are common in the fundamental teachings of Buddhism. In fact, these ideas call for faith, which in the West is suggestive of religion.

FAITH

At this point, faith is essential. Why? Because to become receptive to the activity of dharmakāya, one must intuitively affirm its existence even though one has not yet experienced it. From the side of the dharmakāya, there is inexhaustible power dedicated to the welfare of all sentient beings. Although there are many doors to this power in Mahāyāna practice, the key to all of them is faith in dharmakāya.

An analogy often given by Tibetan Buddhists is that of a very bright sunny day, with the sun beaming down in all directions. The rays of the sun are like the dharmakāya, a power that is always inexhaustibly present. But whether or not dharmakāya affects one's life depends on an individual's attitude, which is likened to a bowl. If the bowl is upside down—that is, if an individual has no faith— then no light gets in no matter how bright the sun of dharmakāya. But as soon as the bowl is turned upright, the bowl is filled with light.

Seen in this context, the Mahāyāna meaning of taking refuge in the Buddha is very broad. It is not merely taking refuge in a historical being who passed away, although it is that also. In addition it is taking refuge in this dharmakāya, which is present and active right now.

Looking back to the preceding discussion concerning the role of conceptualization in understanding reality, faith now appears as an active agent in constructing our experienced reality. This is not to say that we bring the Buddha or the dharmakāya into existence through our beliefs. But if we lack faith, then dharmakāya is excluded from our conscious reality. If we open our hearts to faith, we transform both our perception of the world and our conception of the world.

From the Mahāyāna point of view, dharmakāya is the infinite awareness of all Buddhas, and it is also the source of compassion for all sentient beings. For the people for whom Buddhist teachings are not appropriate, dharmakāya manifests in non-Buddhist ways, fulfilling their needs.

Now, taking refuge in the Mahāyāna tradition becomes a subtle matter. It begins, of course, with the historical Buddha and his teachings that lead one on the path of full spiritual awakening. The Buddha, to Mahāyānists, is a reality that can be experienced right now. As one removes the obscurations from one's own mind, they say, one will increasingly be able to experience the Buddha in daily life.

Even today, people continue to have visions of the Buddha and receive teachings from him—it is an ongoing process. The Dalai Lama speaks about this in his book *Transcendent Wisdom*, saying that from the Mahāyāna perspective it is possible to encounter the Buddha now every bit as vividly as people encountered him in the flesh 2,500 years ago.

OUR GUIDE ON THE PATH

In the Mahāyāna tradition we take refuge in three things: in the Buddha, in the Dharma (his teachings), and in the Saṅgha (the spiritual community, especially the āryas within it). We also take refuge in our spiritual mentors. Most of our own teachers may not be fully enlightened. Like ourselves they are travelers on the spiritual path, although they may have attained a greater degree of insight. They are competent teachers who are able to lead us farther along the path, and knowing this, we take refuge in them and rely on them.

As stated earlier, in the individual vehicle the teacher is regarded as a representative of the Buddha who guides us to the experience of nirvāṇa. In the Mahāyāna tradition the view of the spiritual mentor is very different, a difference rooted in the idea of dharmakāya, the transcendent consciousness of the Buddha. From this point of view a spiritual mentor is a vessel for the expression of dharmakāya. Insofar as a spiritual mentor expresses the dharmakāya within, that person is a manifestation of true Buddhahood.

The idea of dharmakāya is especially useful when we have to deal with the possible faults of our teacher. The subtle but significant distinction here is that we are not saying all spiritual mentors are realized Buddhas, but rather we are regarding them as if they were windows through which we glimpse the dharmakāya.

This has several implications. For one thing, if we should ever become aware of a teacher's faults, we must remember that the teacher is not a static object but a matrix of experienced events, inextricably linked to our own perceptions and conceptions. When we realize this, we may have to take some responsibility for the failings we see in others. There is growth and understanding here, when we start to look deeply at the question of how much a teacher's seeming faults come from his or her side at all, and how much they come from our own side.

If we look upon the spiritual mentor as if he or she were expressing dharmakāya, then when we see a fault, say narrow-mindedness, we can recognize it for what it is. For one thing, as stated above, we can realize that the quality may be within us also, and learn from the way we perceive it in someone else. Or upon deeper reflection, we may conclude that the judgment of narrow-mindedness was purely our own projection, stemming from our own confusion.

Do we have to stand in judgment on our teacher? The answer is no. Our task is to transform and awaken our own minds for the sake of all sentient beings. Our teacher's apparent imperfections, within the context of an understanding of dharmakāya, are simply tools we can use to complete that task.

BUDDHA-NATURE

We are now in a position to consider the meaning of Buddha-nature. In the Mahāyāna context one frequently encounters the statement that all sentient beings, including humans, are endowed with Buddha-nature. This Buddha-nature is variously described as the potential for full awakening, or as the essential perfection of each sentient being, that is temporarily hidden by the veils of delusion.

These teachings are based in part on the *Uttārātantra*, which deals with this subject at some length.

In this text, three reasons are given why all sentient beings have a Buddha-nature. The first of these is that dharmakāya pervades all sentient beings. The second is that emptiness is undifferentiated and is the ultimate nature of all phenomena. And third, all sentient beings have the potential for full awakening.

Exactly what is the Buddha-nature? The *Uttārātantra* declares that the presence of the Buddha-nature, or this essential quality of the mind, is responsible for our discontent with suffering, and is also responsible for our desire, effort, and aspiration for freedom. We know we all want to have happiness and be free of suffering, but why? According to this view the basis is the Buddha-nature, which is the fundamental motivator.

One of the most common analogies used to describe the Buddha-nature is space itself. This analogy has three aspects. First, just as space is omnipresent and yet is unpolluted by everything it pervades, similarly, Buddha-nature pervades every sentient being without being in any way tainted. Second, just as galaxies and universes arise and pass within space, so do the characteristics of our personalities arise and pass within Buddha-nature. Our sensations arise and pass away; Buddha-nature continues. Third, just as space is never consumed by fire, so this Buddha-nature is never consumed by the "fire" of aging, sickness, or death.

According to Mahāyāna, the Buddha-nature is the essential nature of our own minds. It is also referred to as *primordial awareness, extremely subtle mind,* or *original mind.*

Two Aspects of Buddha-nature

Buddha-nature has two major aspects: one aspect is discovered, while the other is developed. With regard to the first of these, it is said that each of us has an essential, beginningless nature that never perishes. And this essence, hidden though it seems to be from our normal understanding, is the source of infinite wisdom and compassion.

This point is illustrated by the following analogy. Imagine a very poor man living in a decrepit little shanty, the only thing he owns in the world. What he does not know is that just beneath his shanty, but hidden in the dirt, is an inexhaustible vein of gold. As long as he remains ignorant of his hidden wealth, this pauper remains in poverty; but when he attends more closely to his own dwelling, he is bound to discover his own fathomless wealth. Similarly, all we need to do is unveil our own nature, and we will find an inexhaustible source of wisdom, compassion, and power. It is nothing we need to acquire, from anywhere or anything. It has always been there.

Seen in this light, the Buddha-nature requires no additions. One does not have to memorize sūtras, recite prayers, or accumulate virtues to create it. All one needs to do is unveil it.

This aspect of Buddha-nature which unveils itself is the dharmakāya. Dharmakāya is undifferentiated, noncompartmentalized, and omnipresent. When one's own Buddha-nature is completely unveiled, one's own mind is revealed as dharmakāya, and the dharmakāya one experiences when becoming a Buddha is not intrinsically separate from anybody else's dharmakāya. This has been likened to the sea dissolving into a drop of water. The awareness of a realized person merges with dharmakāya, but the person's identity is not lost. Continuity of consciousness is maintained.

The second aspect of Buddha-nature is developed and perfected by means of spiritual practice. Here the analogy of a seed is often used. As a seed has the potential of growing into a great and glorious tree, so also can this Buddha-nature grow into Buddhahood. But unlike a seed, the Buddha-nature cannot be destroyed. It is simply there, always present, ready like a seed to sprout when it is brought into contact with appropriate conditions. Those germinating conditions are such things as beneficial spiritual teachings and practices, a spiritual mentor, that is, those conditions which enable us to practice.

Now we encounter one of the more puzzling questions about all this, which is: How can the Buddha-nature be essentially perfect, yet be in need of being "developed"? The answer may be one of perspective. In other words, whether we see the Buddha-nature as complete and perfect in itself with no need for development, or whether we see it as evolving and ripening toward Buddhahood, may not be a matter of the Buddha-nature itself, but how we perceive it.

If we look at this question from the point of view of Buddha-nature itself, we might conclude that it is not evolving. It has no need to evolve, for it is already taintless from the perspective of the fully awakened quality of a Buddha. But if we regard Buddha-nature from an ordinary human perspective, we recognize that we have obscurations that need to be dispelled through spiritual practice. And as we make progress we see that the obscurations lift, and our minds become purified. From this point of view we might understand the Buddha-nature as evolving.

There may be a parallel here with two perspectives on the Buddha's own enlightenment. From the perspective of the individual vehicle, he was not a Buddha until his very last lifetime, 2,500 years ago, when he attained Buddhahood. There was a point, early in the morning when he was thirty-five-years old, when this man achieved spiritual awakening.

From the Mahāyāna point of view we get a quite different picture, that is, that the Buddha was already a fully awakened being when he was born. In his incarnation as the historical Buddha he appeared to strive diligently, to practice austerities, and to find the middle way; but the whole time he was simply "manifesting" the deeds of a Buddha. From the perspective of sentient beings, he appeared to attain spiritual awakening through diligent effort; but from a transcendent perspective it would appear he was enlightened throughout the course of his practice here in this realm.

We must initially take the existence of Buddha-nature on faith, but it can be aroused, made manifest in our daily lives. How? One crucial element is the cultivation of great compassion, which is grounded in the understanding that all sentient beings are alike in terms of their essential nature. Buddha-nature also can be realized by meditatively penetrating into the most fundamental nature of our own minds. Together with compassion as a crucial formative element, arousal of the Buddha-nature then opens the door to the bodhisattva's way of life, which is directed toward enlightenment for the sake of all sentient beings.

13

CULTIVATING A SPIRIT OF AWAKENING

The aspiration to achieve spiritual awakening for the sake of all sentient beings is an ideal at the very core of the Mahāyāna path. Called *bodhicitta* in Sanskrit, and translated as the *spirit of awakening*, its cultivation is the key element that brings one to Buddhahood. We have previously discussed various types of discursive and nondiscursive meditation, all of which are useful in cultivating a spirit of awakening. In addition, however, it is very helpful to engage in devotional practices, which nurture one's spiritual discipline much as water nourishes a garden. One may have a seed, soil, sunshine, and warmth, but without moisture, a seed will remain in the dry ground without germinating. Similarly, without the moisture of devotion, other practices may prove to be quite barren.

According to one Tibetan story, there was once an eminent Lama giving teachings on meditation, during which he explained discursive and nondiscursive meditations concerning various profound topics. But every day, before he started his teachings, he would lead four or five hours of devotional practices and everyone would either have to join in or wait.

Frustrated with this, one of the more learned monks pulled him aside, saying, "You know, we are already quite familiar with these devotional practices. Couldn't you just abbreviate them so that we could spend more time on the important material?"

The Lama looked at him penetratingly and said, "You can do what you want. If your interest is purely in intellectual knowledge, do it your way. But if you wish to gain spiritual realization, I suggest you do it my way. It is these very devotions that make this form of spiritual practice effective."

The practice I shall discuss here is known as the Seven-limbed Devotion, here drawn from verses found in Śāntideva's *A Guide to the Bodhisattva's Way of Life* (*Bodhicaryāvatāra*). These verses are frequently recited and contemplated in Tibetan Buddhist practice.

THE SEVEN LIMBS OF DEVOTION

The first verse we will look at is not one of the seven limbs, but instead, a preliminary verse of taking refuge. It states:

> Until I come to the heart of awakening
> I take refuge in the Awakened Ones.
> So, too, do I take refuge in the Dharma
> And in the community of bodhisattvas.

The first phrase, "heart of awakening" refers to the enlightenment of a Buddha. The next, taking "refuge in the Awakened Ones" can be understood in different ways. *Causal refuge* means taking refuge in someone else, in another person who has achieved enlightenment. Taking refuge in this other person helps to cause, or bring about, awakening, hence it is called *causal*. *Resultant refuge* means taking refuge in oneself, in the Buddha one will become. At the same time this is also taking refuge in the Buddha-nature, in one's own essential untainted goodness.

Now, the first of the seven limbs, which expresses homage:

> With bodies as numerous as all the atoms in the universe,
> I bow to all the Awakened Ones
> Who appear in the three times,
> And to the Dharma and the supreme community.

"With bodies as numerous as all the atoms in the universe": this is an identification with all the bodies one has had in all previous lives, and with all the bodies one will have in all one's future lives. Homage, putting oneself in the lower position, is the key here. It places one in a fertile state of mind. That is what the first limb of this devotion is about, namely, cultivating oneself as if one were a fertile valley.

The Tibetans have a wonderful analogy for this. They look at a person who holds himself above others, believing he is better than others and knows more, and the Tibetans say that person is like someone sitting on a mountain top: it is cold there, it is hard, and nothing will grow. But if the person puts himself in a lower position, then that person is like a fertile field.

The second limb is one of offering:

> To the Victorious Ones and their Children,
> I eternally offer all my bodies.
> O Supreme Beings, accept me fully.
> With reverence I shall be your servant.

The Victorious Ones are the Buddhas, who have gained victory over the distortions and obscurations of their own minds. Their children are the bodhisattvas, those who will become Buddhas.

The next limb has three verses, and is known as disclosure of evil:

> To the perfectly Awakened Ones and those
> Who possess the spirit of awakening and great compassion,
> Who are present in all directions,
> I pray with folded hands.

> Throughout the beginningless cycle of existence,
> In this and other lifetimes,
> I have unconsciously perpetrated evil
> And caused others to do so.

> Oppressed by the deceptions of bewilderment,
> I have rejoiced in those deeds.
> Having seen the error of my ways,
> I earnestly disclose them to the Protectors.

This section focuses on disclosure of the unwholesome through the recognition of one's past bad deeds. Here we reveal these past unwholesome deeds to all the Buddhas. In a sense, we are also addressing our own Buddha-nature, acknowledging that in the past we have engaged in unwholesome actions and even rejoiced in them, but now we are recognizing those actions for what they are. It is important to recognize that there is no suggestion here of guilt. We look upon events or actions, we recognize them as errors, and we let go of them.

The fourth limb concerns rejoicing in virtue and its fruits:

> With gladness I rejoice
> In the ocean of virtue of the cultivation of the spirit
> Which brings about the well-being of all creatures,
> And in the deeds of service to sentient beings.

Here we rejoice in our own practice that generates compassion and loving kindness, as well as service to others; and we rejoice in others' virtues and practice.

The fifth limb requests that the Dharma continue to be revealed:

> To the Awakened Ones in all directions,
> I pray with folded hands:
> For sentient beings who are confused in the darkness of
> suffering,
> I beseech you to light the lamp of Dharma.

The sixth limb requests the Awakened Beings to remain:

> To the Victorious Ones who consider passing into nirvāṇa,
> I pray with folded hands:
> Do not leave this world in blindness,
> But remain, I pray, for countless eons.

We are asking here for the Buddhas themselves to respond to our spiritual needs. Awakened Beings are active for us, not for themselves, and it is appropriate and worthwhile to make such a request.

Finally, the seventh limb of dedication of merit:

> By whatever virtue I have collected
> With deeds such as those,
> May all the suffering
> Of all sentient beings be dispelled.

This directs the spiritual power one has accumulated in all directions for the alleviation of the suffering of all sentient beings.

THE MONASTIC APPROACH TO GREAT COMPASSION

If we look in the classical Buddhist texts for methods of cultivating bodhicitta, we are likely to find discussions like those in the eighth chapter of Śāntideva's *A Guide to the Bodhisattva's Way of Life.*

In essence, the chapter is a monastic's approach to cutting off mental attachments for the purpose of cultivating bodhicitta. Śāntideva recommends what might be called a strictly contemplative approach: overcoming and discarding all one's own attachments, retreating to the forest for a life of solitude, and then from that isolation generating bodhicitta. It is an austere, monastic approach, but it does work, and that is why it has been taught for so long.

In this eighth chapter, Śāntideva makes a strong point of undermining romantic attachments. Using the most graphic terms he tries to discourage sensual attraction to the opposite sex, calling a woman's body a bag of flesh filled with nothing but organs and excrement. (A Buddhist nun would of course be taught to look at the male body in the same way.) What Śāntideva is trying to do here is to banish from the listener's mind any vestige of attraction to romance, and especially sexuality, and wipe the slate clean for the development of bodhicitta.

The Tibetan tradition presents two approaches to cultivating compassion. The first is this monastic approach, which is well-suited for cultivating evenness of mind. As a monk one has no spouse, no children, so one may be less inclined to cherish some people and reject others. The monk removes himself from human attachments and treats everyone with equanimity. It is a situation conducive to developing universal loving kindness and compassion.

The Lay Approach to Great Compassion

Tibetan Buddhism also presents a lay approach to cultivating compassion for the practitioner who is actively engaged in society, who may have a spouse and children as well as many other accumulations of worldly life. Although such a lifestyle often aggravates attachments and other mental distortions, those relationships also contain great potential for spiritual growth.

Most of our intimate human relationships contain attachments mixed with love and compassion. One reaction to this, as we have discussed, is a to pull away from such relationships, to go into solitude and focus on developing love and compassion for all beings equally. The alternative is to decide to stay in the relationships and refine them, recognizing there is much of profound value in those relationships, even if they are mixed with mental distortions. This situation is a fertile ground for cultivating discrimination, particularly between attachments and pure loving kindness and compassion.

In a romantic relationship there is usually a strong element of attachment, but there also is love and affection. Having cultivated a selfless, loving concern for another person's well-being, the next step is to develop this toward others, eventually embracing all sentient beings with even-mindedness. This is the foundation for great compassion.

The monk starts his spiritual path by withdrawing from human society, and from that vantage point he spreads out his cherishing to include all sentient beings equally. Lay practitioners may start by cherishing those within their families, then gradually extend that attitude to encompass all living things. If this does not happen, then the family simply remains a close-knit unit separated from the rest of sentient beings by a fortress of self-centeredness. However, if it does happen, this expansion of cherishing can be an important path to awakening.

Śāntideva gives a marvelous analogy for this expanded sense of cherishing others. He suggests that we cultivate a view of ourselves and others as being limbs of the same body. If the neck itches, for instance, the hand does not feel like it is doing the neck a favor when it reaches up to scratch it. That is because there is something connecting the two that is deeper than the individual identities of the hand and the throat, namely, the awareness of the whole body.

One might quite reasonably counter, "That's a nice idea, but it's not true among people. I can be depressed all day, while Scott is filled with good cheer. We're not all of one body. We're different." To this response Śāntideva recommends that one experience suffering without projecting one's sense of "my-ness" upon it, but rather simply recognize it as suffering, without any inherent owner. The essential question here is: What makes my suffering mine? Śāntideva suggests this is because we have habituated ourselves to identifying with the suffering we experience directly. However, it is also possible to empathize with suffering that we know only inferentially.

As we investigate this through deep meditation, we find that the feelings and thoughts we experience are mental events, arising and passing, but they are not identical with ourselves any more than our shoes or clothes are. Normally we identify with those thoughts and feelings, and it is this identification that makes them seem more important than others' states of mind.

At this point we might protest: "Wait a minute, I already have plenty of problems of my own. Now you want me to identify with one other person or even with many other people."

It is true that expanding our circle of identification with others also increases our own potential for a certain type of suffering. A mother may love her children so much that if they meet with adversity, she may suffer terribly. If we expand this identification to include all beings, it seems to expose us to vast suffering, because there are so many beings.

If we isolate ourselves in our individual lives, saying we are not going to fall in love, get married, or form bonds with others because that creates more suffering, we may end up with another kind of suffering instead, the suffering of isolation. The difference is that isolation is a sterile suffering leading nowhere, while suffering that comes from empathizing with others is a path to Buddhahood.

Although it may be true that broadening our circle of identification increases a type of suffering, this does not necessarily mean our lives get harder. As our compassion grows, the sense of identification with all life is enhanced. And as wisdom deepens, our more conventional understanding of suffering is transcended as we penetrate through it to the unprecedented joy of insight into the nature of ultimate truth.

SELF-CENTEREDNESS

The opposite of great compassion is self-centeredness. A key concept in Buddhism, self-centeredness is the attitude that one's own well-being is more important than anyone else's. Since childhood, we have all known what this means: if there is something nice that another person and I both want, I should get it and not that other person.

As we become adults and our vision of the world gets larger, we develop concentric circles of self-centeredness. At the core is the original idea that my own well-being is of paramount importance. Around that is the next circle: my spouse, my children, best friends, people whose self-interest I also cherish because they are vitally important to me. The next circle is comprised of acquaintances, people I only marginally care about. Around this are the vast number of people whose well-being I do not care about at all, toward whom I am indifferent. Finally, there are the people whom

I perceive as obstructing my own well-being. My self-centeredness demands that these people encounter nothing but adversity. Hence, the self-centered mind considers these people as enemies: if they meet with misfortune, that is good; if they benefit, that is bad.

We can live a life based on self-centeredness, and at first glance this appears to work to our advantage. If there is a piece of cake that I want, self-centeredness says I should get it. If I push someone else away and I get the cake, I get the pleasure of eating it and the other person does not. If I am competing with others in the office, self-centeredness may help me get the higher position, or get the raise. It looks every time like self-centeredness is an ally, because it helps me to get what I want.

But what happens to us on a deeper level, what does self-centeredness do to our sense of well-being? For starters, it sets us at odds with the rest of the world. If others also are basing their lives on self-centeredness, then we are immediately in conflict with everyone else. This leads to disharmony, struggle, and friction. Superficially, self-centeredness may look good, but it turns out to be a great source of misery for individuals and society. Self-centeredness pits nations, cultures, and religions against one another and is a major cause of the world's suffering.

An alternative to self-centeredness is cherishing others more than ourselves. If we consider the welfare of each person equal to that of any other, it follows that the well-being of all other sentient beings is of immeasurably greater importance than one's own individual welfare. When this altruistic attitude is combined with wisdom, it counters the problems of self-centeredness and of misguided affections that can result in such afflictive situations as co-dependency. If we want to know the effects of self-centeredness, Śāntideva says, look at the suffering and fear in our own lives. To see the results of cherishing others, he continues, look at the lives of the Awakened Beings, who embody great compassion.

GREAT COMPASSION

The practice for the eradication of self-centeredness corresponds closely to the practice for cultivating great compassion. Like the earlier loving kindness meditation, this practice moves sequentially from ourselves, to loved ones, and to the greater sphere of living things. But there is a significant difference here. In the former loving kindness practice we brought another person to mind as someone external to ourselves, and wished for that person to be happy and free of suffering. But to develop great compassion we do something radically different. Instead of looking at a person from the outside, we shift our perspective to theirs, as if we were looking out through their eyes.

We now shift our perspective and develop loving kindness for other people as if we were they, taking into full account all of their human attributes. This takes some imagination, so it is helpful to be specific, thinking of the person's real fears and desires.

We shift to the other person's perspective, generating loving kindness for that person from that person's own point of view. As the practice deepens we use the one-pointed mind as a tool to look deeper, mixing the generation of loving kindness with a clearer vision of the person's own fears and desires. And gradually we find that even if that person's expressions of the wish to be happy and avoid pain appears to be very different from our own, at the root they are the same.

We start this process with people we are very close to, gradually shifting to people toward whom we are indifferent. Eventually we move to people we find completely repugnant. But even in this case we do not look at these offensive people from the outside, wishing that they be happy as in loving kindness meditation, but instead we try to see their situation from their own perspective. Looking from the others' viewpoint, we can begin to realize they also are trying to be happy, just like all other sentient beings, though they may be going about it in a very confused way. Even if their behavior is extremely unwholesome, we may be able to penetrate to the roots of their actions so deeply that we recognize their innermost desires and yearnings are identical with our own.

In this way we shift the axis of our priorities and cultivate a feeling of cherishing others more than ourselves. This becomes more than a meditation; it becomes a life-transforming attitude that expresses itself in action.

What can we do to alleviate the suffering in the world? Pursuing this question may lead to great compassion, which is based on this sense of even-mindedness toward all living creatures. This is more than the wish "May you be free of suffering"; it is taking upon ourselves the task of alleviating the suffering of others, and of bringing others to a state of well-being.

When generating this great compassion we must remember that the "I" that takes this on is beyond the level of personality, otherwise this path can develop into a kind of altruistic ego trip. To avoid this, we need to go deep into the nature of our own being, to the Buddha-nature. We can look at this task and ask ourselves, "How can we hope to relieve all sentient beings from suffering when we cannot even do it for ourselves?"

The answer here is that our limitations are not immutable, and they can be overcome. To manifest great compassion in the world, we may decide we can best serve others by being a doctor or politician, even president, but the essential thing is to become a Buddha.

We need to become a Buddha, an Awakened Being, and then we can become a Buddha doctor, a Buddha Dharma teacher, or a Buddha farmer—whatever we want to be. This is the only way to achieve maximum effectiveness.

14

TRANSFORMING MISFORTUNE
INTO THE SPIRITUAL PATH

BODHICITTA

The spirit of awakening, or bodhicitta, arises from a compassionate concern for all beings, expressing itself in the aspiration to be of the greatest possible benefit to all beings through the achievement of the complete spiritual awakening of a Buddha. We become bodhisattvas when this motivation arises effortlessly and spontaneously out of great compassion, when the sense of cherishing others more than ourselves comes naturally. It is at this point that we truly enter the Mahāyāna path to Buddhahood.

As we explore the Buddhist path, it appears that all of its theories and practices can be understood as preparation for bodhicitta, as the actual cultivation of bodhicitta, or as results of bodhicitta. So bodhicitta is really the very heart of what the Buddha taught.

As we engage in these Buddhist practices, we can say that in a sense they all require effort. All are intended to align our conscious mental activity, our conscious behavior, with that which would naturally flow if our Buddha-nature were unobscured and unveiled. We build up to that through practice, and gradually we align our conscious state of mind with the Buddha-nature. And when it gets aligned, our loving kindness arises spontaneously, rather than coming with effort from the conscious mind.

Buddha-nature is aroused through great compassion, compassion that breaks down the barriers of separateness between sentient beings, and dissolves any sense of superiority we may have toward others. Some of us may be more intelligent or more attractive than others, and some of us less so, but beneath those distinctions we are fundamentally alike in that we are all rooted in Buddha-nature.

From this profound sense of identity with other sentient beings, the next step seems natural: taking upon ourselves the goal of freeing all sentient beings from suffering.

When we transcend effort and great compassion starts to arise spontaneously, then very swiftly the Buddha-nature itself becomes spontaneously evident. Once bodhicitta becomes effortless, one becomes a bodhisattva. And as soon as one becomes a bodhisattva, it is said one has attained a facsimile of full enlightenment, of Buddhahood.

The attributes of Buddhahood have been mentioned before: boundless compassion, wisdom, power, utter spontaneity of effortless action. And this effortless action is always directed toward the benefit of all sentient beings. A bodhisattva is a living facsimile of Buddhahood; not yet a Buddha, but displaying many attributes of a Buddha.

THE LIVES WE LIVE

The ideas discussed above may seem impossibly idealistic to many of us. We might like to be bodhisattvas, but instead we are consumed by the trials and disappointments life often brings us. For this reason, it is important to learn how to transform the valleys and peaks of life into spiritual growth. Nearly all of the material that follows is based on a text by a great Nyingma Lama named Dodrupchen, the third of that name, who passed away in 1926. He was a very profound Dzogchen master, with deep insight into the nature of primordial awareness.

Dodrupchen himself calls this text *Transforming Felicity and Adversity into the Spiritual Path.*[22] Here Dodrupchen starts out on familiar ground; the human propensity to dwell on the negativities of our lives. When reviewing a day, many of us tend to remember vividly only the unpleasant things, the misfortunes. Even after meeting with someone just briefly, we may then spend hours dwelling on every single slight, every single uncomfortable circumstance we feel we have encountered.

The more we disregard the power of our own attitudes, and instead blame our suffering and dissatisfaction on factors outside ourselves, the more the world appears to us as hostile. We become paranoid, we suffer from an illness of the mind. In addition, the more we become consumed by these negative attitudes, the more we actually attract negative circumstances to us, Dodrupchen says.

Many of these attitudes focus on other people, and on what we perceive to be their faults. Every day it happens: someone does something that displeases us in some way, and we become obsessed with that person's faults. That obsession is a perverse sort of meditation, a form of one-pointedness, but not one that does anybody any good. These two patterns of mentally dwelling on other people's faults, and speaking of other's faults, can only harm us. They bring us internal grief and disharmony, and create conflict in our relations with the people around us.

Instead, we can radically shift our attitudes toward the events of our own lives—troubles, suffering, irritations—we have always considered misfortunes. We can simply shift our attitude 180 degrees and no longer regard them as essentially harmful or undesirable.

TRANSFORMATION

Transforming our attitudes concerning adversity is a rich and powerful subject, the key to the rest of this chapter. As a beginning, we can prepare ourselves with contemplation before misfortune even arises. By understanding the spiritual transformation adversity can bring, we can develop an inner courage and enthusiasm, a sense of almost looking forward to adversity. This is sometimes called a "warrior attitude," referring to a person who is well prepared, well armed, and who likes a good challenge. But the battle here is not against another person nor a physical situation, but is instead a matter of transforming a difficult life condition into something of spiritual benefit.

A first step toward better understanding is realizing that nearly every time we express irritation or hostility we are expressing ignorance. When we encounter something that upsets the mind we can return to that wonderful maxim from Śāntideva: "If the problem can be remedied, why be troubled about it? If the problem cannot be remedied, what is the point of fretting over it?"[23]

The essential point is transforming misfortune into the spiritual path, and gaining satisfaction from that. To do this we can acquire a number of skills, tools of attitude that are long established.

Renunciation is the first tool. Misfortune may have arisen in our lives, some suffering may have occurred, and this is a good time to look closely at our reactions to those events and probe the roots of those reactions. If we ask what the source of this suffering is, we may find attachment there and decide this attachment is not worthwhile. Instead, we can develop a stronger sense of renunciation, of decreasing our attachment to the external affairs of this brief life—gain and loss, good and bad reputation—and replace these with more meaningful priorities.

Taking refuge is another powerful tool for transforming adversity. In times of insecurity, when we need guidance or are experiencing great grief, taking refuge in the Three Jewels—the Buddha, the Dharma, and the Saṅgha—can be very powerful. It can greatly deepen our practice.

Here is an example of the power of refuge. The teacher Ku-ngo Barshi, who gave me instruction on the *Seven-point Mind Training*[24] of Chekawa, was a layman, the only lay teacher I had during my fourteen years as a monk. He was a very benevolent, good man. He was also a fine scholar, a teacher of poetry and Tibetan grammar, and he was probably the best teacher of Tibetan medicine living in his time. Moreover, he was very learned in Buddhist theory and practice.

In Tibet Ku-ngo Barshi had been an aristocrat, wealthy with land and an extended family. But during the course of the Chinese invasion of Tibet he suffered greatly, his land was taken, and many of his family were executed or virtually enslaved. Forced to flee for his life, he arrived in India as a pauper.

When I met him he was an old man, living in a little shanty. He was working full time, for the equivalent of about thirty dollars a month, teaching Tibetan medicine. He told me once that when he was in Tibet, he had maintained a spiritual practice but was rather casual about it. It was easy to coast in Tibet at the time; life was comfortable, with lots of Dharma and with many spiritual adepts around.

It was only when his life became difficult, he told me, that his practice became truly rich. He had lost all the physical supports on which he had relied earlier in his life—his wealth, his position, his family—and now he had only the Three Jewels in which to take refuge. The effect? I know how he appeared to me: extremely soothing, very calm, with a gentle good cheer that seemed to saturate his person. He truly took refuge in Dharma, and his spiritual presence deepened.

Through taking refuge we cultivate humility and remove arrogance, which is a tremendous obstacle to spiritual practice. It is hard to be arrogant when we are terribly sick and in great pain, or when we have just gone bankrupt or have lost someone we love. These are times to take refuge.

Refuge and renunciation, to return to the warrior analogy, are both weapons for transforming adversity into sources of satisfaction. There are many such tools, and the more tools we master, the more adept we will become at coping with the adversities of life by embracing and transforming them.

Transforming adversity is an area of Dharma where our spiritual practice really transforms our daily lives. We can begin modestly, by accepting events and transforming small degrees of adversity. We can start, for instance, with the person at work who is unhappy, disgruntled, and who has a tendency to be insensitive. Instead of reacting to this person and letting his or her qualities consume our minds, we can choose to respond in a way that does not make us become unhappy ourselves.

The alternative, quite simply, is unhealthy. Responding to life's adversities with mental afflictions such as anxiety, resentment, and rage creates illness. These reactions are imbalances of the mind, and because the mind is intimately related to the body, all these reactions are physically unhealthy. If we are in good health they make us sick, and if we are sick they make us even sicker.

WHERE IS HAPPINESS?

A crucial element of transforming adversity into spiritual growth is stated succinctly by Dodrupchen: "The mind is the complete source of our happiness."

Few of us live as if that is true, and yet it is. There is an essential ingredient of happiness that is not found at the stimulus end of our experience, in the things we experience, but instead at the receptor end. That ingredient is the mind. The pleasure seemingly found in an experienced event actually reflects the unique qualities of mind of the person having the experience, rather than any quality intrinsic to the object of experience itself. All the external things we do may act as catalysts for the happiness we seek, but the happiness really arises from our own minds.

POTENTIAL PITFALLS

It may seem surprising, but transforming felicity into the path can be a far more difficult matter than transforming adversity, with more potential pitfalls. For example, if we are feeling great and everything is going excellently, we may become complacent and begin asking ourselves, "Who needs Dharma?" Padampa Sangye, a great Indian Buddhist contemplative who taught in Tibet about a millennium ago, addressed this very point. He said, "People can cope with a lot of adversity, but only a little felicity."

Another danger of good fortune is laziness. This is not laziness in the usual sense of low energy, but rather a spiritual apathy that manifests when we apply ourselves, even quite strenuously, to meaningless activity. This form of laziness lies in our failure to choose worthwhile applications for our energy.

How then do we transform our attitudes so we do not become enchanted with good fortune and be made complacent or lazy by it? Here are two themes discussed by Dodrupchen.

The first is meditation on impermanence. The idea here is not to turn felicity into adversity. Instead, the object is to deeply realize the fluctuating, transient nature of all the phenomena we are enjoying. The result will be that our enjoyment of good fortune will still arise, but intoxication with it will not. We will remain clearly aware that our new possessions will inevitably wear out and be thrown away, and even our human relationships, precious as they may seem, will change and eventually disappear.

The second theme is meditation on contentment. This can be part of loving kindness meditation, where we begin by directing loving kindness toward ourselves. From this beginning we can look at what we seek, on the deepest level, and shift from there to considering what we really need, and what we already have. Point after point, we will find we have more in our lives than we thought.

As Dodrupchen says, the reason why contentment is so important is that lack of it can block our spiritual practice. Discontent can make us so restless we have no will to practice Dharma, while too much good fortune can divert us so thoroughly we never find the time or will for practice.

If we learn to transform adversity into spiritual growth as well as transform our felicity into practice, then gradually we will learn to continue our practice, no matter what the conditions.

THE NATURE OF ADVERSITY

Now that we have some ideas about how to transform adversity into the path, we can look deeply into the actual nature of adversity. If a sudden event arises, and as a result of that we experience unhappiness, most people would call that adversity. But what if we find that because of this "adversity" and subsequent suffering, our spiritual practice is somehow enhanced, in a definite causal relationship? Is this still adversity? Most people automatically assume there is something inherently miserable about adversity, that it is obvious to everyone what adversity is and what it is not. We feel adversities are self-defining and that we are only unwilling recipients of them.

However, Buddhist teachings say adversity is something quite different. Rather than being a purely objective condition it is related to the subject, the perceiver.

As the ideal of bodhicitta and the role of spiritual practice become central to our lives, these teachings can begin to come alive. On the other hand, insofar as we still do believe our well-being hinges on external circumstances, the idea that adversity is not self-defining may not be very relevant. If we believe adversity is determined solely from the objects' side, then in a sense it is, because we have relinquished our own ability to influence the matter.

As we start to shift our thinking, it becomes obvious that whether or not we identify something as adversity is up to us. As we develop more and more tools for transforming events, we stop defining events as felicity or adversity. Instead they simply become events, and far less likely to be obstacles to the spiritual path.

Let us take another step. Is it possible to cultivate the attitude that the present circumstance, no matter what it is, is ideal for our well-being and for our spiritual practice? This attitude is useful in a very practical way, as we develop Dharma practice. It requires a deep understanding that each event as it occurs, moment-by-moment, is a powerful stimulus for some facet of our spiritual growth. Each moment is perfect for the practice and may provide us with an opportunity to cultivate intelligence, compassion, stability, equanimity, renunciation, or patience. Psychologically, this is an utterly life-affirming stance in that it exercises our energy, our intelligence, our enthusiasm to transform our lives in a thoroughly wholesome way. Spiritually, this attitude may be enormously helpful in opening up the transforming power of our Buddha-nature.

15

EMPTINESS AND FULFILLMENT

Wisdom, the wisdom of realizing the emptiness of inherent existence of all phenomena, is a central theme of many Mahāyāna teachings. This perhaps can best be symbolized by a hand *mudrā*, or gesture, that is among the most common mudrās in all of Buddhism. It is the mudrā that is used in meditation, the left hand palm up beneath the right hand, with the thumbs touching. The left hand refers to wisdom, to the realization of emptiness, while the right hand symbolizes compassion. The message here is that wisdom provides the basis for compassion; the latter cannot flourish without the former. Like these two mental qualities, the hands do not just rest on top of each other passively but are integrated. They join together where the thumbs touch, representing the unique integration of wisdom and compassion.

For many people in the West, Buddhist practice really starts with cultivating an understanding of emptiness. This has been emphasized in the teachings of His Holiness the Dalai Lama, who points out that emptiness teachings may be the best way for many people to attain confidence in the full range of Buddhism. That is because emptiness can be investigated with one's intelligence without resorting to a leap of faith. As one begins to understand emptiness, faith may also arise. And from faith other qualities may be cultivated more easily, including compassion, devotion, and loving kindness.

THE REAL LOCATION OF THE PERCEIVED WORLD

To approach an understanding of the lack of inherent existence of phenomena, let us begin with the question: Where do the objects that make up our experiential world truly exist? As a starting point, let us consider an object we are becoming very familiar with— this book. All readers would agree, I think, that the pages of this book are white. But what is this whiteness? The essential point to be made is that the book's whiteness that we perceive is contingent upon our own perception.

We need not go into a lengthy discourse on the functions of the retina, optic nerve, and brain. The essential thing to realize is that any act of sight is a result of complex interactions between the object being seen and the sensory faculties. Vision is an emergent event, not some little window through which images and colors stream in to a passive receptor.

If one were a bee, for instance, one's perception of this page would be very different than it is for a human. Similarly, it would look uniquely different to a bat, an owl, or a snake. Each of these creatures has unique visual faculties that condition the visual perception of the page.

Even among the readers of this book there will be subtle differences in how we see a page. Our eyes may vary, some with astigmatisms that distort the vision, others with conditions that variously alter the image. We may light the book in various ways, or hold it at different angles; for each of us a unique flux of visual imagery constantly changes within our field of vision.

A visual field, roughly an oval space that contains this book and whatever other objects are around it, is in front of each of us at this instant. What each reader sees while reading this book is unique, and dependent upon that person's unique faculties.

Our visual perception does not exist in our absence. If there is no visual faculty, the perception and the perceived visual object do not exist at all.

This raises an interesting question. If we are looking at a man named Scott who is eight feet away and wearing a brown coat, where is the brown coat that we see? Our immediate response is that it is eight feet away, but the truth is that the perceived attributes of the coat, such as its color, exist only in relation to our sense faculties. If the coat, with all its perceived qualities, truly exists eight feet away, this would imply that our senses are somehow able to project these attributes through eight feet of empty space.

Let's take another example. If we go out on a clear night and gaze up at the stars, we can see stars hundreds of light-years away. We gaze out there and see a tiny white dot, but the star as we perceive it is dependent upon the visual faculties with which we are seeing it. The perceived star would not exist without someone to see it. Is the star that we perceive out there, many light-years away, or is it somewhere else? The idea that it is out there is obviously absurd, for it would imply that our eyes are able to condition something hundreds of light-years away.

To make it more absurd, the star is not there where we see it anyway. The star has moved since its light started journeying across space hundreds of years ago, and the place where we see the star may be nothing but empty space.

If perceived objects are not out there in front of us somewhere, where are they? Searching our bodies for these objects is equally fruitless. There is little doubt that the act of seeing requires a complex series of neurophysiological events, but that does not mean these perceived objects are somewhere inside our heads.

While seeing a red rose, specific areas of the brain may need to be activated for this perception to take place, but this does not imply that the perceived rose is actually in the brain. Even if one had a wonderful microscope with which to look into the brain of a person who was seeing a rose, that microscope would not find a tiny red rose anywhere. The same is true of our other faculties, of smell, taste, and touch, and so on.

Similarly, we also have the impression that sound is out there somewhere, but this too collapses under closer scrutiny. We can say the sound of snapping fingers is produced by the fingers, but is that where the sound is? The physical basis of sound consists of oscillations in the atmosphere, traveling at about 650 miles an hour, but if there are no ears around, there is no perceived sound to be heard. The oscillations may ripple off walls or shatter buildings, but without the essential ingredient of an auditory faculty to sense them, those oscillations are not perceived sound but only oscillations. The experience of hearing is a dependently related event, produced in part by our auditory faculties.

In every instance of sensory experience, our sensory faculties are contributing something. If we go to a concert and hear wonderful music, our experience of that music is inextricably related to our own hearing. If we look at a painting, the same is true. All sensory experiences are dependently related events involving both external physical events and our own sense faculties' interaction with them.

We usually do not act as if experiences really are dependently related events. Most of the time we treat sensory phenomena as if they are exactly what they seem to be. We hear sounds and we say, "What a noisy place!" never considering what role a listener might play. This process is called reification, in which we imagine something to have a substantiality, or tangibility, that it in fact does not have. Through reification we ignore the subjective contributions to an event, seeing it entirely as an objective entity.

From the *Madhyamaka* view, or the Centrist view of Mahāyāna Buddhism, reification is erroneous, because the way things appear is not how they exist. This is, in essence, what is meant by the Mādhyamaka assertion that the phenomenal world is dreamlike. All perceived objects are conditioned by our sensory faculties and by the mind.

The dream state we experience during sleep is similar. In a dream we may seem to live in an environment, we may seem to have a body and emotions and all kinds of sensory experiences. In a dream our body and all of its experiences are entirely mental phenomena, but while we are having the dream we do not realize this. Instead we reify the experience, as if it were a purely objective reality.

WHAT IS REALLY THERE?

Having determined that the reality we perceive depends on our sense faculties, what then really does exist outside of our senses? When we close this book and leave the room, shutting the door behind us, what remains? It is an ancient question, that has been asked since the time of the Greeks. What exists behind appearances, what really exists out there?

This brings up a familiar problem: What happens when a tree falls, and nobody is in the forest to watch it or hear it? Most people agree something happened; the tree trunk is on the ground, there is a big dent, things start to rot, and ants and termites live in the fallen trunk. But what happened?

Western scientists have traditionally responded to this question by trying to find primary, or intrinsic, qualities of the falling tree that can be measured. Mass is one of those, the idea being that the tree has a quantifiable amount of stuff to it. Speed is another quality that does not seem to depend on anyone's perception.

Briefly considering the history of Western scientific thinking on this point may be a useful digression that may help us better understand the nature of emptiness. Also, by examining our cultural assumptions about the nature of reality we can better understand and penetrate those assumptions, and by so doing, come to appreciate the Buddhist view.

Since Galileo took his telescope and turned it on Jupiter, scientific thought has increasingly depended on the power of mechanical instruments. We get the sense—and it is widely promoted by science—that by using mechanical instruments and mathematics we stop being subjective and instead become objective.

Everybody knows the senses can be misleading, it is said, so let us dispense with the senses. They are giving us only appearances anyway, and we are trying to penetrate through those. The idea of objective measurement came to be strongly emphasized during the time of Galileo, and by the end of the nineteenth century, scientists felt the objective science of physics was virtually complete. The physics of the time was assumed, with very few exceptions, to be an absolute representation of what was really out there.

At the beginning of the twentieth century, this view began to break down. Scientists started to understand more clearly that their instruments of measurement were themselves contributing to the data they were detecting. But the real revolution came with the development of quantum physics, which investigates the very smallest components of physical reality. It is here that the participatory nature of measurement and experimentation becomes most obvious.

In quantum mechanics, attributes of mass, speed, shape, and location vanish as purely objective entities. All of them can only be seen in relationship to the methods of measurement. As the renowned physicist Werner Heisenberg said, "What we observe is not nature itself but nature exposed to our method of questioning."[25]

As scientists looked still deeper, they also started questioning the objectivity of the analytical tools they use. Mathematics, for instance, is one more human creation. Euclidean geometry is only one of a theoretically infinite number of geometries that can be used, and the same goes for algebra, and for various logic systems.

The subjective element seems to be inescapable on all fronts. In no facet of science, whether we are dealing with astronomy, physics, or medicine, do we get even one bit of information about any reality existing independently of our modes of questioning.

All of our sensory experience consists of appearances that are contingent upon our sense faculties. Even by reducing everything to the subatomic level of electrons, quarks, and so forth, we are still left with nothing but appearances. What is inescapable is that all we know of the world, theoretically and empirically, consists of appearances to the mind. We have access to nothing else.

Understanding this, the concept of reification becomes universally applicable. In the same way that we look out on the world, and view perceived objects as if they existed inherently in objective space, so too do we view things like electrons and sound waves as if they existed independently of our conceptions of them. Perceived objects exist in relation to our perceptions of them, and conceived objects exist in relation to the conceptual schemata within which they are understood. We reify an object by removing it from its context, by ignoring the subjective influences of perception and conception.

MIND

At this point we might draw the conclusion that since all known phenomena are contingent upon the mind, only the mind is inherently real. So then, what is the mind? As we investigate this question, we find ourselves reifying the mind just as we reify everything else.

To cut through this reification, let us consider a moment of awareness within a continuum of consciousness. That moment's past has vanished, and its future has not yet come. But when we try to conceptually isolate the moment's present, we see the same continuum of time again. The moment we thought was in the present also has a beginning and an end.

As we continue this process, searching for the present between the beginning and the end, the present instant of awareness becomes infinitely immediate. Any mental event becomes unfindable. The mind turns out to be ultimately unfindable. It is not in the past, it is not in the future, and it is not truly existent in the present. If we subject it to this form of "ultimate analysis," it just vanishes.

We also discover that the mind has no location. We can find no compelling reasons for locating the mind in our heads, or anywhere else. Awareness itself has no shape, no color, no size, and no location in time or space.

Consider a moment of awareness, the mental event of perceiving a shirt as blue. As we look deeply into this event, we find no evidence this perception exists independent of the shirt's blue-ness. The mental event of perceiving the shirt as blue could not exist without a shirt; the event is not self-existent. As the perceived blueness of a shirt is a dependently related event, dependent upon one's visual faculty, so, too, is one's visual perception and mental awareness of the blue dependent on that color.

So even the mind turns out to be no more substantial, no more intrinsic, than any physical phenomena. It is dependent on factors around it in time and space, as are physical phenomena, and likewise, has no inherent nature.

This very absence of an inherent identity, or self, is what is known as emptiness. All phenomena are empty in that they lack an intrinsic nature that exists in and of itself. Physical phenomena, the mind, the self—all of them are empty, all are dependently related events.

From a Buddhist perspective, emptiness is far more than just an interesting idea, one among many. The Buddha and the greatest Buddhist sages and contemplatives have all probed the nature of suffering, especially the mental afflictions of ignorance, hatred, and desire. All of these, they say, stem from the ignorant reification of ourselves and other phenomena.

Reification is the root of all our ills, dividing our sense of self from everything else. Once that division is made, the next step is attachment to "my" side, to what I mistakenly believe is inherently mine. From this springs hostility toward whatever seems to come in conflict with my side, with me and what I think is mine. This root ignorance gives rise to confusion, to attachment, to hostility, and to all the other mental afflictions such as jealousy, conceit, arrogance, and selfishness. The antidote, then, is to experience the emptiness of all phenomena, and to recognize their nature as dependently related events.

A MEDITATION ON EMPTINESS

A very straightforward meditation on emptiness comes from the *Seven-point Mind Training* by the Tibetan contemplative Geshe Chekawa.

We start the practice by pondering the nature of emptiness. With the motivation of deeply changing our experience of reality, we recognize that everything we are experiencing, sensory or otherwise, is just a series of mental appearances. None of them, not even the mind, exist in and of themselves, but are only a matrix of dependently related events.

We gaze out at the room around us, and realize that what we see does not exist independently out there. Next we bring people to mind, all the people we know, realizing that each person also is just a mental appearance. Dwelling upon that, we begin to recognize that we ourselves are only mental appearances. Our bodies, our faces, our personalities, all of these are appearances of the mind, with no intrinsic existence.

Then, Chekawa suggests, just relax. Come to that clarity and then relax in that clarity, without grasping onto, or reifying, anything. When we let go of grasping, we come to a deep conviction that all things are empty of intrinsic existence. Then we relax the mind into a state of clarity—without agitation, without grasping, without dimness, and abide in this realization of emptiness. If a thought arises, we direct the awareness right to the awareness itself, and just abide there.

The point of this practice is to alter our experience of reality, to be able to counter the ignorance that lies at the root of all forms of delusion, hostility, and attachment.

After arising from this meditation, we try to sustain this quality of seeing all things as empty of intrinsic existence. As we go to fix lunch, for instance, we bring to that activity an awareness that our experience of the world is dreamlike. It may seem to exist entirely out there, but the truth is that we participate in that reality, we help create it. As much as we can, we keep this understanding alive throughout the day.

In summary there are two truths, the ultimate truth of emptiness and the relative truth of conventional reality. On the one hand, emptiness is said to be the sheer absence of any intrinsic nature in any phenomenon. This emptiness is the ultimate nature of all things. On the other hand, phenomena also have a conventional reality, the day-to-day truth of appearances we live with. The two, ultimate truth and conventional truth, are finally of one nature. To realize the nonduality of these two truths is a central feature of the culmination of the Buddhist path and the fulfillment of the spiritual quest.

16

The Diamond Vehicle of Tantra

The first chapters of this book focused on the individual path, based on the fundamental teachings of the Buddha. The emphasis there was on our mental distortions and unwholesome behavior, how these are rooted in ignorance, and how this ignorance creates suffering and unhappiness. In terms of practice, the emphasis was on countering these ignorant tendencies.

As we shifted to the Mahāyāna, there was a greater emphasis on the cultivation of wholesome qualities as a way to align ourselves with our own Buddha-nature. These qualities included loving kindness, the stabilized mind, bodhicitta, and the cultivation of wisdom. All of the above are included in what is called the *causal vehicle*, a term derived from the idea that all of them are causes for attaining enlightenment.

MIRED IN SELF-IDENTITY

Implicit in the causal path is an ordinary sense of self. But as we work with the sense of self-identity implied on the causal path, we may find at some point that it inhibits our spiritual practice.

The problem is, that by approaching spiritual work with this ordinary sense of self, we may continue to identify with the unwholesome characteristics we encounter within ourselves. If we have the sense we are not very good people, not very loving people, not very patient people, our identification with these qualities can stymie the entire process of unfolding. To acknowledge the presence of our own unwholesome tendencies is an essential component of self-knowledge; but to become fixated on these same tendencies and to construct our sense of personal identity on that basis can be emotionally and spiritually crippling.

This can become especially crucial in the early years of practice. We may start out with a reasonably good self-image, feeling we are pleasant people, well-liked, basically all right. Then, as we start meditating and become more aware of how our minds are actually operating—what motivates us to get through the day and how we regard other people—we may become increasingly aware of the chaos that is actually in our minds. We try to meditate for a weekend, and find our minds are virtually uncontrollable. Worse, when our minds do slow down, we find they are absorbed in trivia or unwholesome fantasies.

If we identify with this conditioned mind as it reveals itself, we may develop a sense of ourselves as rather disgusting individuals. This can become a major obstacle to enlightenment.

The more we gain insight, and see just how tenacious many of these qualities are, the more we may feel enmeshed and bound by them. This sense of being trapped by our darker qualities does not stop just with us; it can include our spouses, people we work with, everyone we encounter. The whole world can appear in a dismal light, seemingly because of the spiritual practice we have embarked on.

THE QUICK PATH

In contrast, the Tantric path is one of complete and radical transformation of our self-identity. Tantra builds upon some of the key ideas we have explored in previous chapters. One of these is the essential purity of the mind, which is called *Buddha-nature*, or *tathāgata-garbha*.

The idea of Buddha-nature is that the essential nature of the mind is infinite purity, fathomless joy, power, wisdom, and compassion; right here, right now. We do not have to earn our Buddha-nature or become enlightened to have it. We have it right now, and it is common to all sentient beings.

Paralleling Buddha-nature, the infinite potential of each individual, is dharmakāya, the omniscient, omnipresent awareness of a Buddha. Dharmakāya is called the Spiritual Body of the Buddha, and is inseparably related to the Buddha-nature. Both of them are active, eternally dynamic.

The causal path is a step-by-step, or gradual approach to realizing our potential to become Buddhas. According to the Buddhist account, this path of cultivating virtues while maintaining one's present sense of ordinary, conventional identity takes three "uncountable" eons of time. An uncountable eon in the Buddhist sense is far longer than science's estimate of billions of years from the Big Bang to the Big Crunch (assuming that the universe oscillates through these cycles). A Buddhist eon is longer than that, and it takes three uncountable eons on the causal path to achieve enlightenment.

The idea of having to wait this long to become enlightened can seem daunting. But focusing on the sheer span of time misses the point. If one is earnestly following the bodhisattva way of life, it is meaningful to remain in the cycle of existence in the service of sentient beings.

The other approach, the radical transformation of Tantra called the *resultant vehicle*, may take only a few lifetimes. The essence of the Tantric path is a radical shift in identity, a real leap. In one leap, we shift our perspective and identify with the Buddha-nature, instead of with our previous conception of an ordinary self. In the time of a finger-snap, we drop our previous identification with our limitations, and instead identify with the essential nature of our own being. We are without beginning, without end, undefiled by any distortion.

THE ROLE OF DESIRE

The Tantric attitude toward desire is profoundly different from everything we have discussed before. In earlier chapters, when we considered the individual and Mahāyāna paths, we looked at desire as something to be calmed. From this point of view, desires have no benefit; they keep us in saṃsāra and suffering. But in Tantra we transform our attitude toward desire by accepting and transmuting it, for desire has tremendous energy.

In the individual vehicle there is something of a hard-nosed attitude, regarding attachment as thoroughly afflictive. The promoted ideal is to become a monk, and avoid desire entirely. This entails developing renunciation, including the abandonment of relationships that are tainted by attachment. The Mahāyāna approach is somewhat different. It acknowledges attachment as a mental distortion that leads to grief and needs to be rejected. However, intimate relationships need not always be abandoned, for they may be avenues for developing positive attitudes such as loving kindness and compassion, which are the central pillars of Mahāyāna practice.

In Tantra we actually use the energy of desire to move us along the path. We accept this energy, we transmute it, and we do not try to stifle it. For this reason, Tantra may be practiced effectively while living an active life with spouse, children, and job. This has been true in Tibet, where many of the greatest Lamas have been lay people with families.

THE GURU AS THE BUDDHA

The relationship between Guru and disciple takes on another dimension in Tantric practice, in addition to those we have already discussed. To review, on the individual path we regard the Guru as a representative of the Buddha. The Guru's personality is of little consequence, because the Guru represents the Buddha, like the emissary of a king. On the Mahāyāna path, we look upon the Guru as if that person were a Buddha. We do not look upon him or her as a fully realized Buddha, but with full recognition of that person's

Buddha-nature. While we may be aware of the Guru's faults, we simply do not become fixated on them; instead we focus on the Guru's virtues as expressions of the Buddha-nature. We regard this person as a vessel for the blessings and inspiration of the dharma-kāya, and therefore as a facsimile of a Buddha.

The Tantric view of the Guru is quite different. First of all, the qualifications are very high for a person to be a genuine Tantric Guru. In this context the Guru is seen not as an emissary as in the individual path, nor a facsimile of a Buddha as in the Mahāyāna path, but as an actual Buddha, having the same degree of realization, of compassion, of purity, as the historical Buddha.

A key to this Tantric view is the understanding of the lack of inherent existence of oneself, other people, and one's environment. Realizing the lack of inherent existence of the self, and intuitively affirming his Buddha-nature, the Tantric practitioner designates himself as a Buddha on the basis of his Buddha-nature, which is ultimately undifferentiated from the dharmakāya. In a similar fashion, he identifies his Guru as a Buddha on the basis of that person's Buddha-nature.

Intuitively affirming the immanent presence of the dharmakāya makes one receptive to very deeply transformative blessings from this divine source. And placing one's faith in a human teacher can also bring about very swift blessings. If one can integrate one's faith in the dharmakāya and one's human teacher, this makes one receptive to powers of spiritual transformation that are both profound and rapid. This is the reason for looking upon the Guru as a Buddha.

In his book *Introduction to Tantra*, Lama Thubten Yeshe makes a very important related point. The chief reason for cultivating such a relationship with a Guru is to awaken our own internal wisdom. The outer Guru is simply a way to stimulate the inner Guru. We should keep in mind that we must identify ourselves as Buddha in exactly the same way we regard a Guru as Buddha.

THE PRACTICE OF TANTRA

The gateway to Tantra is initiation, known to Tibetans as *empowerment*. The core of an empowerment is a meditation, shared between the Guru giving the initiation and the student receiving it. The Guru teaches the meditation, Guru and student participate in it together, and a transference, or a form of communion, takes place.

The point of the initiation is to catalyze certain potentials that will then come to fruition, if the practice is followed. The degree to which the initiation takes hold depends upon the teacher's realization and the student's spiritual maturity. If these two are well-primed the initiation can be very powerful, a life-transforming event.

In the Tibetan Buddhist view, initiation is essential. One can read about Tantric practices in books, but unless one has been initiated, those practices will be ineffective at best, and they may actually be quite harmful.

Each initiation is for a certain meditation deity, called a *yidam* in Tibetan. Deities like Avalokiteśvara, Mañjuśri, or Tārā may each be regarded as an archetype embodying a different facet of enlightened awareness. These are not truly existent, separate entities existing in some divine place. Avalokiteśvara, for instance, is said to be the manifestation of the Buddha's compassion. And most Tibetans consider His Holiness the Dalai Lama to be an embodiment of Avalokiteśvara in human form.

The identification of yidams as archetypes, however, must not conceal the fact that they are often referred to as divine persons. This is illustrated by the Buddhist account of Avalokiteśvara, who long ago pledged to put off his own spiritual awakening until every sentient being had reached enlightenment. It is said he actively served beings for eons and eons, but that finally he gazed out on sentient beings, limitless in number, and realized there were still limitless beings in suffering. Seeing this, he wept in despair. From his eye a tear fell, and from that tear arose Tārā, a yidam in feminine form. Tārā turned to Avalokiteśvara and said, "Don't despair, for I will help you." Avalokiteśvara and Tārā are thus regarded as persons, but, like ourselves, they are viewed as being devoid of inherent identity.

From the Tantric perspective, the habitual clinging to ordinary appearances and conceptualizations is the ignorance shrouding our Buddha-nature. Once the problem is understood, the Tantric response is radical. Unlike the causal path, which responds to each form of ignorance with an antidote, such as countering anger with loving kindness, Tantra instead leaps beyond this ordinary view. In Tantric practice we transcend conventional appearances by using our imaginations to visualize our own forms as the divine form. With Tārā or any other deity as one's yidam, these visualizations are very specific, with every aspect of the deity's form, posture, hair color, and ornaments well described and full of symbolic meaning.

In Tārā practice, for instance, we use our imaginations in two ways. On the one hand we look upon our Guru as Tārā, as a manifestation of Buddha-nature, and on the other hand we visualize ourselves as Tārā. It does not matter at all if we are man or woman; in either case we visualize ourselves as Tārā in a feminine form.

Such a practice may sound like a self-generated illusion, like retreating from a world that is too tough and creating a world of spiritual fantasy instead. But for Tantric adepts the imagined world of Tantra is no more devoid of inherent existence than ordinary reality, but it acknowledges a deeper, divine reality that transcends ordinary appearances.

There are two aspects to this practice. The first is imagination, in which we visualize ourselves as a yidam, whose body is one of light, permeated with joy, of uttermost purity. Tantric teachings emphasize that each one of us has a subtle body in addition to our gross physical body. The subtle body, composed of vital energy, operates in tandem with the gross body. This is where Tantric

Buddhism introduces the subtle body's system of the different *cakras*, or energy centers, as well as *nāḍis*, or energy channels.

As we visualize ourselves as a Tantric deity, we are actually transforming this subtle energy body by the very act of visualization. If we visualize ourselves as Tārā, for instance, we mold our subtle energy bodies into Tārā. We are taking reality and we are shaping it, transforming it.

The second aspect of Tantric practice is known as "divine pride," which follows from the first. In response to the question "Who are you?" the Tantric practitioner may answer, "I am the Buddha Tārā." We are not pretending or wishing to be Tārā, but simply acknowledging our essential purity right now, identifying fully with our Buddha-nature in the form of Tārā. Through this process of transformed visualization and identification, we become aware of the limited ways we usually conceive of, or "imagine," ourselves.

Without an understanding of emptiness, the practice of visualizing oneself as Tārā and imagining oneself to be Tārā is sheer fantasy. But with such understanding, the practice of visualizing ourselves in a different form and identifying ourselves as an enlightened being helps us see more clearly what we are not. It gives us much greater clarity about the ways we already identify ourselves in a limited and arbitrary fashion. Through this process, we recognize these limitations as mental distortions and, at the same time, realize that we no longer must identify with them. This is the radical shift of Tantra.

FURTHER TANTRIC PRACTICES

In Tantra the practitioner fully acknowledges both the wholesome and unwholesome events that take place in the mind, neither identifying with them nor being repulsed by them. Wholesome and unwholesome mental conditions are seen as simply arising from prior events, and the practitioner focuses on the essential purity of the Buddha-nature that underlies and enlivens both.

In this context of practice we say that even the mental distortions arise from Buddha-nature. The point is not to repress these distortions, but to acknowledge them and then take their energy and transform it. In Tantra every bit of energy, whether it seems positive or negative, is used on the path. This includes the powerful energy of happiness, which we transform into the path as well. We do that by not becoming attached to it. We do not take happiness as something ultimate, but simply allow it to arise and let its energy flow unimpeded. Problems arise only when we become attached to seeming sources of happiness. We cling to them hoping they will last, and in the end we stifle them.

For Tibetans, Tantric practice is the crowning glory of the Buddhist path, the "express train" to enlightenment. But as Westerners, as members of another culture, we must keep the importance of the Tantric path in perspective in two ways.

First, the Tantric path may be the culmination of the Tibetan Buddhist path, but that does not mean it is somehow more important than other aspects of the path. *Every* part of the Buddhist path—from the most basic moral precepts, to open-hearted loving kindness, to the most subtle understandings of emptiness—has its own unique value. Without a deep realization and practice of moral precepts, the Tantric path can spiral out of control and become detrimental. Without a realization of emptiness, Tantra's use of visualizations and imagery is nothing but fantasy. It is all an interconnected web.

Second, the Tantric path is a path and not to be confused with the actual goal of realization. Tibetans regard Tantra as the fastest route to Buddhahood, but that does not mean it is the only one or the goal itself. Even within Mahāyāna Buddhism there are other paths, such as Zen, that are so different from Tantra that their common roots in the teachings of the Buddha can be difficult to recognize. The crucial point is not to grasp onto one path or one school as being superior to others, but to practice those teachings that most clearly bring about benefit for ourselves and others. This is the pragmatic, altruistic spirit that suffuses Tibetan Buddhism from the ground up, and it is especially relevant in this pluralistic modern world in which we seek to fulfill our essential yearning for spiritual awakening.

NOTES

1. Śāntideva, *Bodhicaryāvatāra*, ch. 1, vs. 28. All translations from the Sanskrit and the Tibetan are my own, unless otherwise indicated.

2. Tib. 'Brom-ston rgyal-ba'i 'byung-gnas (1008–1064).

3. *Bodhicaryāvatāra*, ch. 2, vs. 34–5.

4. For a more detailed discussion of the above issues, see my *Choosing Reality: A Contemplative View of Physics and the Mind* (Boston: Shambhala Publications, 1989).

5. *The Tibetan Dhammapada: Sayings of the Buddha*, transl. by Gareth Sparham (London: Wisdom Publications, 1986) ch. 31, vs. 10.

6. ibid., ch. 31, vs. 11.

7. *Tattvasaṁgraha*, ed. D. Shastri (Banaras: Bauddhabharati, 1968) 3587.

8. *The Tibetan Dhammapada*, ch. 31, vs. 27.

9. ibid., ch. 10, vs. 9.

10. For a detailed discussion of the Tibetan Buddhist practice of dream yoga, see *Ancient Wisdom: Nyingma Teachings on Dream Yoga, Meditation, and Transformation*, by Gyaltrul Rinpoche. (Ithaca: Snow Lion Publications, 1993).

11. *Bodhicaryāvatāra*, ch. 5, vs. 47–48.

12. Takpo Tashi Namgyal, *Mahāmudrā: The Quintessence of Mind and Meditation*, translated and annotated by Lobsang P. Lhalungpa (Boston: Shambhala, 1986) p. 27.

13. ibid., p. 27.

14. ibid., p. 173

15. ibid., p. 30, quoted from *Abhidharmasamuccaya*.

16. ibid., p. 152.

17. ibid., p. 162.

18. Bhadantācariya Buddhaghosa, *The Path of Purification* (*Visuddhimagga*), trans. by Bhikkhu Ñāṇamoli, fourth ed. (Kandy: Buddhist Publication Society, 1979) ch. 9, vs. 8. I have slightly modified the translation.

19. ibid., ch. 9, vs. 37. Quoted from the *Anguttara Nikāya*, vs. 342.

20. See Soma Thera's *The Way of Mindfulness* (Kandy: Buddhist Publication Society, 1975).

21. Buddhaghosa Thera, *The Satipaṭṭhāna Sutta Vannana of the Papañcasudani*, in *The Way of Mindfulness: The Satipaṭṭhāna Sutta and Commentary*, trans. by Soma Thera (Kandy: Buddhist Publication Society, 1975) pp. 80-81.

22. This text is translated with commentary in *Ancient Wisdom*, by Gyatrul Rinpoche, et.al. (Ithaca: Snow Lion Publications, 1993).

23. *Bodhicaryāvatāra*, ch. 6, vs. 10.

24. This training is the subject of my book, *A Passage From Solitude* (Ithaca: Snow Lion Publications, 1992).

25. Werner Heisenberg, *Physics and Philosophy: The Revolution in Modern Science* (New York: Harper and Row, 1962) p. 58.

BIBLIOGRAPHY

Goldstein, Joseph & Kornfield, Jack. *Seeking the Heart of Wisdom.* Boston: Shambhala Publications, 1987.

Gunaratana, Henepola. *The Path of Serenity and Insight.* Ithaca: Snow Lion Publications, 1984.

Gyatrul Rinpoche. *Ancient Wisdom: Nyingma Teachings on Dream Yoga, Meditation, and Transformation.* Ithaca: Snow Lion Publications, 1993.

Gyatso, Geshe Kelsang. *Clear Light of Bliss.* 1982. London: Tharpa Publications, 1992.

Hahn, Thich Nhat. *The Miracle of Mindfulness.* New York: Beacon Press, 1975.

Hahn, Thich Nhat. *The Sun My Heart.* Berkeley: Parallax Press, 1988.

His Holiness the Dalai Lama. *Kindness, Clarity, and Insight.* Ithaca: Snow Lion Publications, 1984.

Hookham, S.K. *The Buddha Within.* Albany: SUNY Press, 1991.

Hopkins, Jeffrey. *Compassion in Tibetan Buddhism.* Ithaca: Snow Lion Publications, 1980.

Lamrimpa, Gen. *Samatha Meditation.* Ithaca: Snow Lion Publications, 1992.

Lhalungpa, Lobsang. *The Life of Milarepa.* Boston: Shambhala Press. 1977.

McDonald, Kathleen. *How to Meditate.* Boston: Wisdom Publications, 1992 (1984).

Mitchell, Robert Allen. *The Buddha, His Life Retold.* New York: Paragon House, 1989.

Nagarjuna and Lama Mipham. *Golden Zephyr*. Emeryville: Dharma Publishing, 1975.

Nagarjuna and Sakya Pandit. *Elegant Sayings*. Berkeley: Dharma Publishing, 1977.

Namgyal, Takpo Tashi. *Mahamudra: The Quintessence of Mind and Meditation*. Boston: Shambhala Publications, 1986.

Nyanaponika Thera. *The Heart of Buddhist Meditation*. New York: Samuel Weiser, 1973.

Rabten, Geshe. *Echoes of Voidness*. London: Wisdom Publications, 1986.

Rabten, Geshe. *Treasury of Dharma*. London: Tharpa Publications, 1988.

Shantideva. *A Guide to the Bodhisattva's Way of Life*. Dharamsala, India: Library of Tibetan Works and Archives, 1981.

Wallace, B. Alan. *A Passage from Solitude*. Ithaca: Snow Lion Publications, 1992.

Yeshe, Lama. *Introduction to Tantra*. London: Wisdom Publications, 1987.

INDEX

A

abuse, (verbal), 4, 97, 103, 123

action. *See* karma

aging. *See* old age

adversity, 9, 160, 161; transforming into the spiritual path,
166–170, 171, 172. *See also*
duḥkha; suffering

afflictions. *See* mental afflictions

anger, 9, 26, 57, 59, 60, 80, 95, 98,
99, 103, 119, 123, 132; at the
moment of death, 68; at the
moment of taking rebirth, 71;
loving kindness as antidote to,
124, 191; mindfulness of,
132–133. *See also* hatred;
hostility

animal, rebirth as, 66

antidote: death and impermanence
as, 19; in the practice of mental quiescence, 111, 116; to
anger, 191; to ignorance, 58,
75, 106, 182; to the mental
distortions, 60, 103; to
unwholesome deeds, 101 *see*
four remedial powers

arhat, 76–78, 85, 141. *See also* liberation; nirvāṇa

arrogance (pride), 8, 13, 48, 54,

169; divine *see* divine pride

ārya, 75, 82, 83, 146; -bodhi-
sattvas, 144

Asaṅga, 106

asceticism, 10; Buddha's practice
of, 36

asuras, 66, 67, 73

Atiśa, 108

attachment, 13, 14, 20, 41, 47, 50,
53, 54, 57, 58, 59, 60, 63, 75,
76, 80, 95, 98, 99, 103, 104,
116, 131, 136, 157, 182, 193;
decreasing, in development of
renunciation, 168; functioning
of, 53; ignorance giving rise to,
48, 53, 183; Mahāyāna
approach to, 188; romantic,
cutting off, 157–158; to this
life, 5–6; -s of this life, 9, 37.
See also craving; desire, mental
distortions; three poisons

Avalokiteśvara, 190–191

avarice, 98, 99, 100

Awakened Being. *See* Awakened
One

Awakened One, 35, 154–156, 161,
163. *See also* Buddha;
Victorious Ones

awareness, 9, 27, 36, 37, 51, 53,
58, 62, 64, 76, 78, 103, 122,

C

as basis of mental stabilization, 125; as support for spiritual growth, 92–94; first of three trainings, 86; in Tibetan medicine, 94–95; restraint from unwholesome actions, 91–92, 94–100, 103–104

motivation, 54, 78, 87, 96, 97, 186; for the practice of emptiness, 183; for spiritual practice, 93, 113; of an arhat, 41; of bodhicitta, 165; of Buddha, 33, 38; of a Dharma student, 87; of a Dharma teacher, 87; of the eight worldly concerns, 5–6, 73; of the person of great capacity, 140; of the person of medium capacity, 139; of the person of small capacity, 139; of the spirit of emergence, 79; unwholesome, 2, 97; wholesome, 2, 4, 46, 73. See also intention

mudrā, 175

N

nāḍis. See under energy channels

naraka realm, 67, 71

natural awareness. See awareness

Nechung Oracle, 65

Newton, Sir Isaac, 54

nihilism, 78

nirmāṇakāya, 144. See also dharmakāya

nirvāṇa, 40–41, 43, 66, 76, 78, 85,

126, 141, 146, 156. See also arhat; Buddhahood; enlightenment; freedom; liberation; spirit of emergence

nonduality, 184

nonviolence, as foundation of spiritual practice, 4

nonvirtue, 13, 15, 18, 98, 139. See karma; ten unwholesome deeds; virtue

Nyingma, 166

O

objects of meditation. See under meditation

objective reality, 21, 23–24, 62, 142–143, 172, 178–179, 179–181

offering, 88, 155

old age (aging), 16, 31, 35, 38, 40, 81, 148

omniscience, 78, 185; qualities of, 38–39. See also Buddha; Buddhahood; enlightenment

oracle. See Nechung Oracle

original mind. See under mind

P

Padampa Sangye, 170

pain, 2, 9, 39, 45, 50, 51, 53, 59, 92, 130, 162, 169; as result of unwholesome actions, 34, 67, 80; experience of, at death, 19,